"In *Creating a Culture of Repair: Taking Action on the Road to Reparations*, Rev. Dr. Robert Turner delivers a groundbreaking road map for transformative change. This powerful book offers a comprehensive guide to repairing the deep-seated wounds of systemic injustice, urging individuals, communities, organizations, and institutions to take meaningful action. Turner's approach is both enlightening and actionable, as he explores the intricacies of reparations across individual, social, institutional, and spiritual dimensions. From acknowledging privilege to dismantling systemic racism, each chapter presents a compelling set of actions that can pave the way for genuine repair. This book is a call to action, urging us to confront our past, engage in transformative measures, and collectively pave the way for a more inclusive future. It is my sincere hope that readers, inspired by this work, will join the movement for reparations and contribute to the repair of our society."

—Rev. Jesse L. Jackson Sr., civil rights activist
and founder, Rainbow PUSH Coalition

"Rev. Robert Turner is a person of profound faith who knows that 'faith without works is dead.' In *Creating a Culture of Repair*, Rev. Turner sets forth a thought-provoking road map for righting past wrongs and building a more just, equal, and strong America. The book is full of his wisdom and inspiration. It is an important read that not only elevates his big ideas but also fortifies the spirit in trying times."

—Cory Booker, United States Senator of New Jersey

"*Creating a Culture of Repair* combines unflinching moral reckoning with an approachable and compassionate future-forward vision for social and spiritual transformation that could come only from a pastor's heart. Turner's unique and pragmatic work outlines a path forward for Christians and all people who are choosing to say 'amen' to the fact that reparations are right, necessary, and very possible."

—Jermaine Ross-Allam, Director,
Center for the Repair of Historical Harms,
Presbyterian Church (U.S.A.)

"Turner has given us a visionary road map that can lead us on the right road to repairing the breach caused by centuries of white supremacy in action. This is a vital book for those who want to learn more about the many harms inflicted on Black people in this country and for those of us who want to make reparations but are not sure how to begin."
—Jocelyn Lieu, member, Middle Collegiate
Church Reparations Task Force

"Turner invites readers to journey with him to both yesteryear and tomorrow as he presents one hundred definitive steps to move toward the goal of reparative justice. Turner contextualizes the necessity for reparations through his own lived experiences after moving from his native Alabama, where a member of his family was lynched, to serve as pastor of the historic Vernon AME Church in Tulsa, Oklahoma, and lead it through the one-hundred-year anniversary of the horrific Tulsa Race Massacre of 1921. Bearing witness to the effects of how government-sanctioned lynch mobs and cowardly killers took capital, cash, and profit-earning capacity from Black Americans, Turner invites all who are serious about reparative justice to walk with him on a journey toward reparations."
—Jonathan C. Augustine, Senior Pastor, St. Joseph AME
Church, and author of *When Prophets Preach:
Leadership and the Politics of the Pulpit*

"Turner has created the most comprehensive contribution that demonstrates how reparations can be done in an impactful way throughout American society. His one hundred actions offer something for everyone in order to not only advance the conversation but also enhance the nation's life and provide healing for its people. He offers practical and achievable solutions to address the various realms where harm has been done and concludes that the work of reparative justice will enhance the lives of all Americans and unify the nation under a common banner."
—Jimmie R. Hawkins, Director of Advocacy, Presbyterian
Church (U.S.A.), and author of *Unbroken and Unbowed:
A History of Black Protest in America*

Creating a Culture of Repair

Creating a Culture of Repair

Taking Action on the Road to Reparations

Robert Turner

WJK WESTMINSTER
JOHN KNOX PRESS
LOUISVILLE · KENTUCKY

First edition
Published by Westminster John Knox Press
Louisville, Kentucky

24 25 26 27 28 29 30 31 32 33—10 9 8 7 6 5 4 3 2 1

Unless otherwise indicated, Scripture quotations are taken from the New Revised Standard Version Updated Edition, copyright © 2021 National Council of Churches of Christ in the United States of America. Used by permission. All rights reserved worldwide. Scripture quotations marked NLT are taken from the *Holy Bible*, New Living Translation, copyright ©1996, 2004, 2015 by Tyndale House Foundation. Used by permission of Tyndale House Publishers, Inc., Carol Stream, Illinois 60188. All rights reserved.

Book design by Sharon Adams
Cover design by Kevin van der Leek Design Inc.

Library of Congress Cataloging-in-Publication Data

Names: Turner, Robert R. A., author.
Title: Creating a culture of repair : taking action on the road to
 reparations / Robert Turner.
Description: First edition. | Louisville, Kentucky : Westminster John Knox
 Press, [2024] | Includes bibliographical references. | Summary: "An
 accessible guide for individuals and groups wanting to influence
 significant institutional action while also acting on their own to
 repair the effects of racial injustice in our communities, churches, and
 spheres of influence"-- Provided by publisher.
Identifiers: LCCN 2024000312 (print) | LCCN 2024000313 (ebook) | ISBN
 9780664268077 (paperback) | ISBN 9781646983773 (ebook)
Subjects: LCSH: African Americans--Reparations. | Reparations for
 historical injustices--United States. | Reparations for historical
 injustices--Religious aspects--Christianity.
Classification: LCC E185.89.R45 T87 2024 (print) | LCC E185.89.R45
 (ebook) | DDC 305.896/073--dc23/eng/20240207
LC record available at https://lccn.loc.gov/2024000312
LC ebook record available at https://lccn.loc.gov/2024000313

Most Westminster John Knox Press books are available at special quantity discounts when purchased in bulk by corporations, organizations, and special-interest groups. For more information, please e-mail SpecialSales@wjkbooks.com.

To my maternal grandparents, Henry and Rosetta Birdsong, and my paternal grandparents, Millage Jernigan and Susie Turner Jones, none of whom finished high school yet collectively raised thirty-seven children, two of whom are my parents, Robert and Ruth Turner. I dedicate this book to my ancestors, none of whom have ever received reparations, and to my God, without whom I would not be here today.

Contents

3. Institutional Reparations 71
State and national programs dismantling, repairing,
and making restitution for systemic injustice

4. Spiritual Reparations   143
*Churches and other religious communities atoning
for the sin of racism enacted in the name of God*

Foreword

*I*n 2023, the United States celebrated the sixtieth anniversary of the March on Washington for Jobs and Freedom and the Rev. Dr. Martin Luther King's most famous speech. Although many remember only Dr. King's "dream" from that speech, much of its content actually focused on the nightmare that was the reality of life for tens of millions of Black Americans (a nightmare that still continues today). On August 28, 1963, from the steps of the Lincoln Memorial, the thirty-four-year-old prophetic leader reminded the nation,

> We have come to our Nation's Capital to cash a check . . . a promissory note to which every American was to fall heir. . . . It is obvious today that America has defaulted on this promissory note insofar as her citizens of color are concerned. Instead of honoring this sacred obligation, America has given the Negro people a bad check, a check . . . marked insufficient funds.[1]

More than six decades later, this "bad check" has only gotten worse. Before the COVID-19 pandemic, voting rights were under attack, disproportionately disenfranchising Black people; "tough on crime" policies had led to criminalization and mass incarceration, particularly impacting Black Americans; 26 million (or 61 percent of all) Black people were poor or low-income, and 41 percent of all unhoused people in the "land of the free and home of the brave" were Black.

The pandemic further exacerbated systemic racism and economic inequality, deepening and spreading along the fissures of racism and discrimination that have long been part of these yet-to-be-United States. The 2020 election and subsequent attempted coup by Donald Trump and his enablers led to the greatest attack on our democracy since the Civil War and Reconstruction gave rise to overt racism and violent acts motivated by white supremacy. The American nightmare experienced by Black people has become ever more excruciating.

However, at the same time that poverty and inequality have grown, affirmative action and equal protection under the law have been undermined, and anti-Black policing and policies have been enacted, it does not have to be this way. The promissory note of liberty, justice, and the pursuit of happiness is within reach if only the people, including our communities of faith, governmental authorities, and society at large, have the will to make good on its promises.

Indeed, we should hear the case for reparations in that same speech from the Rev. Dr. King. We must work to make it a reality today. Dr. King continued:

> We refuse to believe that the bank of justice is bankrupt. We refuse to believe that there are insufficient funds in the great vaults of opportunity of this nation. And so we have come to cash this check, a check that will give us upon demand the riches of freedom and security of justice. . . . This is no time to engage in the luxury of cooling off or to take the tranquilizing drug of gradualism. . . . Now is the time to lift our nation from the quick sands of racial injustice to the solid rock of brotherhood. Now is the time to make justice a reality to all of God's children.[2]

Yes. May we make it so. But how?

In the Gospel of Luke, John the Baptist begins a public ministry to prepare the way for Jesus, and crowds start coming to him in the wilderness to be baptized. "And the crowds asked him, 'What, then, should we do?' In reply he said to them, 'Whoever has two coats must share with anyone who has none, and whoever has food must do likewise.' Even tax collectors came to be baptized, and they asked him, 'Teacher, what should we do?' He said to them, 'Collect no more than the amount prescribed for you'" (Luke 3:10–13). After admonitions for tax collectors came admonitions for soldiers.

John's message in Luke's Gospel is squarely about justice and repair, echoing the Hebrew prophets and Mary's Magnificat in a call for the just distribution of resources, equal protection under the law, and repair of the breaches in society.

Fast-forward to today. Individuals, congregations, and the systems and structures of society in the twenty-first century are in need of models answering that question, "What, then, should we do" to be engaged in effective anti-racist, pro-repair ministry and policy? Taken with Dr. King's reminder of the urgency of the moment and the promise of life, liberty. and the pursuit of happiness, Luke 3 provides guidance to all of us on the case for reparations.

These instructions from Luke 3—to share resources freely and abundantly; to act justly and equitably in economic and political matters; and to restore the people, soldiers, tax collectors, and faith leaders into right relationship with one another—echo the recommendations of *Creating a Culture of Repair: Taking Action on the Road to Reparations* by the Rev. Dr. Robert Turner. This insightful and instructive book provides important steps—in fact, one hundred of them—that individuals, communities, institutions, and spiritual authorities can take to atone for the sin of racism and repair the breach of white supremacy.

In the Hebrew Bible, the Lord laments to the prophet Ezekiel, "I sought for anyone among them who would repair the wall and stand in the breach before me on behalf of the land, so that I would not destroy it, but I found no one" (Ezek. 22:30). This book is an invitation to all—individuals, congregations, communities, governmental and other institutions—to be the *one* to stand in the gap.

Because if we ever are to repair the cruel injustice of systemic racism and white supremacy, we must engage in the work of restitution. Let us heed the words of the Rev. Dr. Robert Turner and walk the road to reparations and build a culture of repair.

Liz Theoharis
Kairos Center for Religions, Rights, and Social Justice
August 2023

Introduction

Remnants of Greenwood

A crowd descended on the county jail. Dick Rowland, a young Black man, had been taken into police custody after being accused of sexually assaulting Sarah Page, a young white woman. Hearing of the gathering crowd, armed Black men—many of them veterans of World War I—came with the intention of helping the sheriff to protect Dick Rowland from being lynched, but they were turned away by the sheriff and instructed to go home. Despite ordering away those who aimed to help him, the sheriff left the lynch mob intact. One of the members of the mob tried to take a gun from one of the Black men. A fight ensued. The gun went off, and when the white man who sought to take the gun was accidentally shot in the scuffle, violence erupted.

Over the course of the evening, a white mob moved into the neighborhood of Greenwood, home to Black Wall Street and some of the most successful Black Americans in the country. The mob torched businesses, looted houses, and shot Black citizens in the street. From the air, men in low-flying airplanes fired guns and dropped incendiaries onto buildings. Bodies were dragged through the streets, families executed at point-blank range, babies ripped out of pregnant mothers' stomachs.

The Tulsa Race Massacre of 1921 was the largest act of violence in America since the Civil War. According to the report of the Tulsa Race Riot Commission (not convened until 2001), it was the first time that airplanes were used to attack an American city. Not on September 11, 2001, at the Pentagon and World Trade Center,

1

nor on December 7, 1941, at Pearl Harbor, but on May 31 and June 1, 1921, in the Greenwood District of Tulsa, Oklahoma. During those eighteen hours of terror, ten thousand people were made homeless, six hundred businesses were destroyed, and more than three hundred people were brutally killed, their bodies discarded in mass graves.

I came to Vernon African Methodist Episcopal Church, in Greenwood, after one of the most direct encounters I have ever had with God.

Every so often in my Christian sojourn, God seems to call on me to do more. Such was the case one summer night in early August 2017. In the few months leading up to this call, I felt a spiritual pull from Almighty God to go in a certain direction, but which way I didn't know.

What I knew was that I was feeling a spiritual drying of my brook similar to the prophet Elijah when he was at the Wadi Cherith (1 Kgs. 17). Thus, one night, after going through months of spiritual aridity, I prayed to God, "Lord, I know that you want me to do something, and I want you to know this time I will not fight you. Whatever you want me to do, wherever you want me to go, I say yes to your will. In Jesus' name I pray, Amen!"

When I finished my prayer, I got off my knees and grabbed my phone from the bed to put it on the charger, looking at it to see the time. I noticed that I had a text message. It was from Bishop Michael L. Mitchell, who presides over Oklahoma and Arkansas, offering an opportunity in his district if I would take it. I was astonished that the direction I had just sought from God was delivered instantaneously. And so, as I had made the promise to God to say yes to whatever path he laid before me, I immediately replied to the bishop with one word: yes.

I didn't ask what he wanted me to do or where he wanted me to go. I was going. With that vow I made to God, I committed to Bishop Mitchell to move my family to a place I had never been before. I went forward, not knowing where I would pastor, how much I would make, nor where my family would live. In fact, I did not know any of this information until I arrived in Tulsa on August 26, just a few weeks after that first phone call.

The congregation of Vernon was founded in 1905, the same year many historians say Greenwood, and later Black Wall Street, was formed. From that founding moment, Vernon has been the staple of Greenwood. Our towering steeples have overlooked the parameters of Black Wall Street for nearly a century. Vernon's congregation held Tulsa's first Black principal, first Black attorney, first Black physician, and first Black peace officer. The first children's Head Start program in Tulsa was at Vernon.

As Greenwood prospered, Vernon did as well, and when Black Wall Street saw destruction during the Tulsa Race Massacre, so did Vernon. But as the district survived, so did the basement of our church, the only edifice on Greenwood Avenue that survived the Tulsa Race Massacre. That basement became a refuge to those fleeing violence on the night of the massacre. Leading pillars in the community saw Vernon as their place of spiritual renewal and believed that its revitalization was paramount to the prestige of the Greenwood District. Consequently, as people began to return and make Greenwood great again, so did the members of Vernon.

Following the destruction in 1921, the basement of Vernon was refortified by 1922. The sanctuary began to be rebuilt in 1925, finishing in 1928. The rebuilding of our historic church came with the help of those brave people who chose to stay. Vernon remains the oldest continuous Black landowner of the same parcel of land in the entire Greenwood/Black Wall Street District.

When we think of this massacre, we think about the economic hit for Black people. We think of the tremendous loss of life and of the exodus of those who refused to live among the racism in Tulsa any longer.

We often forget the stories of the people who stayed. The government didn't come to aid the rebuilding of that which they helped to destroy. White churches did not heed the call to rebuild the houses of God. It was none other than the people of the Greenwood community, whose families were murdered and livelihoods destroyed, who decided to stay amid the profound heartbreak and insecurity to rebuild the community in which they once prospered.

Those who stayed created an ecosystem where Black excellence saw a renaissance and more Blacks continued to come to Tulsa in search of their slice of the American pie. The growing Black population attracted more doctors, peace officers, and teachers who knew nothing of the massacre. Consider the economic genius of those individuals who—two generations out of slavery—created the most prosperous town for Blacks in the country in a place that had just become a state in 1907. With no aid or entrepreneurial training, they became first-generation business community and church leaders. The new arrivals ate well from their slice for several decades, yet those who stayed and rebuilt were somehow forgotten in the very community they helped to restore. In a conservative state that prides itself on having little to no government interference, the story of Greenwood should have been highlighted as an example of what a determined people did with no welfare, affirmative action, Pell grants, small business loans, nor philanthropic grants. Instead, the names of those determined people have faded as though they were a victim of their own success, and this important remnant has been forgotten for nearly a century.

Not forgotten at Vernon are the individuals who stayed and rebuilt our church. The stained-glass windows of Vernon display craftsmanship and artistry unlike anything else seen in Black Wall Street. While their physical brilliance is unique, it is the names in each piece of glass that are inspiring. These names reflect those who financially helped rebuild the sanctuary. Individuals such as S. E. Berry, who was one of a half dozen Blacks in Greenwood who owned an airplane; R. T. Bridgewater, the first Black physician in Tulsa; Barney Cleaver, the first Black sheriff's deputy; schoolteachers J. T. A. West and J. I. Wallace; S. M. Jackson, the owner of the most prosperous Black funeral home, which embalmed and buried the only two people who received proper burial after the Tulsa massacre: Rueben Everett and Vernon church member Eddie Lockard.

Dr. R. T. Bridgewater's thriving medical practice was burned down during the massacre; his office safe was pulled out and left in the street. Bridgewater never received anything for his loss, yet he remained, started his practice again, and stayed at Vernon. S. M. "Sam" and Eunice Jackson rebuilt their mortuary business, and today their relatives still run the renamed Jack's Funeral Home. The Jacksons had a child shortly after the massacre who tragically died very young.

The Rev. Alfred Barnett Sr. survived the massacre and later became an ordained clergyperson in the African Methodist Episcopal Church. Lucille Figures survived the massacre and later moved to Texas; her son continues to support the church in her honor. Lucille's granddaughter Patricia Barnett is still a member of Vernon, where she sings in the choir, a stewardess who serves with a glad heart and a loving spirit.

Robert Fairchild knew Dick Rowland personally. He was in high school at the time of the massacre and stayed at Vernon virtually his entire life. He taught Sunday school and opened a dance hall where his love of dance was displayed for all to see. He and a few other businessmen started the Greenwood Chamber of Commerce, which is still in existence today.

Ernestine Gibbs was a survivor who owned several businesses and was a part of the missionary society. Her descendants still reside in the area and are business owners as well. At the time of the massacre, Vernice Sims was on her way to the prom, which, sadly, never happened. Vernice became a prominent spokesman and witness of the massacre who gave her testimony to the Tulsa Race Riot Commission and was included in the lawsuit led by Johnnie Cochran advocating for reparations.

James Wesley Williams and his wife were co-owners of Dreamland theater and Williams Mechanic shop, which was featured in the opening scene of the HBO series *Watchmen*. They also owned several rental properties and a confectionary—all of which were destroyed during the massacre. They never received an insurance claim or reparations. Williams's descendants are still in the area and one is a popular news anchor, Danya Bacchus.

John R. Emerson Sr. owned a cab transportation company, hotel, and other businesses that were decimated during the massacre. He rebuilt it all, but during the midcentury "urban renewal" of the Greenwood area, the hotel was demolished. Today none of his businesses still exist. His granddaughter Harriet Emerson is a member of the church and its board of trustees.

Olivia Hooker survived with her parents, who owned Hooker Clothing. Her family moved away after the massacre, but Olivia never forgot what she saw and endured as a child. She joined the armed forces after obtaining several degrees. It was my great honor in ministry to do her homegoing memorial eulogy celebration at Vernon AME Church. She was the last known survivor from the 1921 Tulsa Race Massacre.

Each one of these families lost the ability to inherit capital, cash, and well-known businesses offering quality products: three elements necessary for building wealth regardless of ethnicity. The loss of capital and cash did not result from poor financial management nor cyclical market conditions. Neither was their misfortune due to one of Tulsa's notorious tornadoes. No, these families lost the right to inherit this capital, cash, and business as a result of it being taken in an act of state-sanctioned terrorism in which vigilantes deputized by the sheriff descended on Greenwood and in less than eighteen hours burned more than thirty-six city blocks to the ground. Wealth gained by those who believed in the American dream went up in flames by those who gave them a nightmare.

Doubly devastating is that while the victims' descendants are doing well and the Greenwood community still exists, it is a shell of its former self and the families for the most part have been unable to recreate the same level of prosperity as when Black Wall Street was in its prime. Those survivors who dared venture back into the water of American capitalism as business owners found more obstacles than did their parents, who had begun their enterprise on land recently seized from indigenous Americans and sold cheap to settlers. The theft of the so-called Oklahoma Territory from the indigenous tribes (who had already been pushed to the area from southeastern states in earlier "Indian removals") was the first of three major incidents of land theft in Oklahoma in less than one hundred years. The second was the Tulsa Massacre of 1921, and then midcentury, through urban renewal coupled with interstate highway construction, the land was stolen again, moving Blacks out to make room for white-owned development. Now the entrepreneurial spirit, though not dead, is not shining as brightly as it once did. Most have chosen to work for someone else. It seems as though, subconsciously, they have collectively decided to shield their genetic entrepreneurial brilliance from those who systematically seek to destroy any development of an autonomous Black economy.

Watching the insurrection at our nation's capital on January 6, 2021, reminded me of what happened here in Tulsa one hundred years before: an angry white mob was causing mayhem with the support of elected officials. The destruction of Greenwood was far worse, of course, but the basic premise holds that white racist mobs in every generation know their privilege and seem hell-bent to use it to the detriment of justice, peace, nobility, and civility. America has yet to show that it is willing, let alone able, to rein in its white racist mobs. Sadly, America's citizens, democracy, and justice will continue to suffer because of it until the country finds the strength to abolish its idol of white supremacy.

Our capitalist free-market system cannot reach its fullest potential so long as it allows white racial terror attacks to go unpunished. The destruction of Black homes and businesses by racial terror in places like Greenwood in Tulsa; Rosewood, Florida, in 1923; and Wilmington, North Carolina, in 1898, meant America lost fortunes overnight. Tragically, there is virtually a Tulsa in every state of the union.

In the summer of 1919 alone, African Americans endured more than twenty race massacres. Black soldiers were just coming back from fighting fascism in Europe and were terrorized at home in a season so bloody it became known as Red Summer. These Black men left their hometowns as sharecroppers and "boys" and returned as privates, sergeants, and captains. Their self-esteem was greater, their knowledge wider, their sense of self deeper—and their tolerance for economic exploitation eliminated. They had looked totalitarianism in the face and defeated it. They returned to never be defeated again. The newfound swagger of these Black men became an affront to those who held to white supremacist ideals.

Those ideals had been promoted during the war years by the movie *Birth of a Nation*. Released in 1915, this silent film depicted Black people as slothful and violent. The chief antagonist was a Black man who was attempting to rape a white woman. Instead of being deflowered by a man who was, in her mind, a "brute beast," the woman jumped off a cliff. Upon hearing about it, white men, depicted as great and honorable gentlemen, banded together to form the Ku Klux Klan to avenge the suicide of the young white woman and crush the supposedly lazy, ignorant Blacks who wanted more rights so that (in the minds of the Klansmen) they could have more access to white women. The Klansmen were applauded for their efforts and presented as the heroes of the film.

Membership in the Klan, which before the film had been dwindling, began to skyrocket. The movie was a major blockbuster, and President Woodrow Wilson had a private screening of it in the White House. After seeing the movie, he reportedly said, "It's like writing history with lightning. My only regret is that it is all so terribly true."

When the highest-ranking authority in the land, the commander in chief, has declared that a movie depicting Black people as lazy and ignorant and Black men as desiring to assault white women is true and accurate, he promotes false propaganda, which grows unchecked. As we saw on January 6, 2021, after Trump and his media buddies had been carrying on about how the election was stolen, lies of this magnitude often lead to violence.

So after President Wilson's comments and the resurgence of the Klan, when these Black patriots returned from the Great War in Europe, the local whites whose identity rested on the pillars of white supremacy, which gave them permission to think that they were better than everybody else, were perplexed. *These "boys" now think they're men? Soldiers? Heroes?* White men were bewildered when they started to see Blacks doing better financially than them. It troubled their mind. Racist whites could not stand to see the truth that Blacks were just as smart, talented, and ambitious as they were. Their fragile minds and poisoned hearts could not handle that, so they had to destroy the evidence of that truth—and that included homes, churches, and libraries. During the massacre of Greenwood, the Blacks who were fleeing overheard whites saying to themselves, "How did we ever let them get this land in the first place?" The problem is they didn't "let them" get anything—Black residents purchased the land with their own money.

Only two things happen when you encounter the truth after being raised in a lie: you either accept the truth and expose the lie, or you eliminate the truth and hold fast to the lie. The people in Greenwood and other predominantly Black communities across the country where there was even a modicum of success were victims of the latter. And to justify their mayhem, racist whites in a majority of the communities that saw a massacre told themselves another lie, an unproven allegation that a Black man had said or done something to a white woman, the principal complaint and concern of the Klan in *Birth of a Nation*, the movie that was praised by President Wilson.

Wilson's belief that *Birth of a Nation* was a realistic representation of Black Americans is appalling. Even worse is that this inaccurate, callous, and racist line of thinking is still common in our public discourse more than a century later. We can see this same resistance to the truth in the present pushback against critical race theory, an academic framework for looking critically at race and the significant role it has played in the United States of America and the world. Individuals expressing their disdain for public education by passing laws and starting petitions against the teaching of critical race theory in K-12 schools are offering pointless solutions looking for a problem. Even advocates of critical race theory will tell you that it is a principle taught at institutions of higher education, not K-12—a fact that shows how detached from reality the opposition really is. However, this fact does not stop them from attacking it, because the core of their objection is that the true history of Black America might be taught and the great white lies of American history might be exposed. These are lies that have been promulgated for centuries, claiming "slavery was not all that bad" and "it was a benefit for Blacks to get them out of Africa," two lies we will explore and expose later in this book.

Modern defenders of these lies think that teaching how this country has harshly treated Black people—while giving advantages to white people that Blacks did not and do not enjoy—is unpatriotic and harmful to children. What these adults mean is that *they* find it uncomfortable and perhaps even threatening. They insist that racism is an aberration in American history, not the consistent theme. They are ignorant to the fact that while the racist laws may be changed or no longer enforced, the racist culture that they created and sustained still remains.

The area of Alabama where my extended family resides is one of the poorest areas in the country. A region known as the Black Belt, it was once one of the most prosperous places in the country, due to its fertile soil on which my ancestors grew and picked cotton.

My family chose to stay in Alabama after slavery even after my great-grandfather's first cousin was one of the last people lynched in Bullock County, Alabama. One way of defeating your enemy is to outlast them, but while we won the land, those who upheld Jim Crow took the wealth.

The case of Greenwood is similar; the Blacks there have outlasted their oppressors, but unfortunately the land now belongs to the city and the wealth has been transferred to seemingly everyone but the descendants. Similar to economics, justice does not trickle down. It must be corrected in order for justice to be done.

Those warriors who braved the aftermath of the worst race massacre in American history—the largest civil disturbance since the Civil War—recreated their community without any help from the government, insurance companies, or nonprofits. They turned their hell into a haven and found a way to make "bricks without straw," as the Israelites did in Egypt (Exod. 5). The people who stayed rebuilt the city of ruins just as Nehemiah rebuilt the wall of Jerusalem. They held their position as Moses held his arms up (Exod. 17), but these brave Black Tulsans did not have anyone to assist them as Moses did. This is why reparations matter.

Reparations are not just about reimbursing victims of assaults like that on Greenwood for the property, income, or even lives lost "back then." Reparations are about the impact that four hundred years of "back then" still have on Black Americans today.

What Are Reparations?

When people think about reparations, they might assume that they personally will have to write a check because of something that happened long ago—something for which they personally bear no responsibility. They might see it as a handout to people who were not directly impacted by the harm done long ago—slavery, Jim Crow, housing discrimination, and so on. However, making reparations is actually repair or redress of an offense. It is society's way of atoning for things it has done and correcting the damage that is still present, even if the damaging acts may have ceased.

Simply put, reparations are not merely given; they are a matter of justice. They are demanded by moral systems as old as Judeo-Christian, Islamic, and Buddhist traditions. For both the religious and nonaffiliated, if you adhere to the Magna Carta or the Declaration of Independence, uphold the Golden Rule or any philosophy of fairness, or believe in the intrinsic value of all people, then your own conscience will recognize that reparations are not merely due, they are past due! Reparations are not charity; they are justice. Reparations are not complementary but crucial to repairing the fabric of our democracy and making the Constitution real for all Americans.

America prides itself in being "one nation, under God, with liberty and justice for all," but as long as we deny justice to African Americans for the atrocities they have faced in this country solely because they are Black, we are not living up to the pledge that each one of us has recited since childhood. That pledge does not say justice for all except enslaved people or sharecroppers or Black people. It does not say justice for all except those who are no longer alive or their descendants. It simply says, "justice for all." Such an august statement is not a whisper but a shout, not a whimper but a flame, not a weak wind but a tornado with the intention to sweep up all impediments to justice and jettison them from our midst.

We as a nation have managed to "strain out a gnat but swallow a camel," as Jesus says in Matthew 23:24. And now we have become sick. We have fussed and fought ad nauseam concerning lighter issues like filibustering, debt ceilings, and mask mandates but have swallowed or ignored the monumental issues such as America's ongoing systemic racism, current-day manifestations of white supremacy, objectification of Black lives, and centuries of compacted harms and neglected redress. America is deliriously ill because it has denied justice and reparations to an immense number of its citizens.

Healing can come only when you first acknowledge you are sick and then take your medicine. Reparations are a vital part of the medicine America needs to take in order to have true racial healing. Considering the immense negative energy America expended to secure, sanction, and uphold slavery, white supremacy, and the dominance of whiteness, the same energy should be exerted positively in repenting, reversing, and repairing those most abominable actions.

The United Nations' general description of reparations says:

Adequate, effective, and prompt reparation is intended to promote justice by redressing gross violations of international human rights law or serious violations of international humanitarian law. Reparation should be proportional to the gravity of the violations and the harm suffered. In accordance with its domestic laws and international legal obligations, a State shall provide reparation to victims for acts or omissions which can be attributed to the State and constitute gross violations of international human rights law or serious violations of international humanitarian law.[1]

The National Coalition of Blacks for Reparations in America (N'COBRA) specifies that the intended recipients of reparations are "people injured *because of their group identity* and in violation of their fundamental human rights by governments, corporations, institutions and families" (italics mine). They are entitled to what "they need to repair and heal themselves."[2]

The Movement for Black Lives makes clear that reparations "cannot be achieved simply through 'acknowledgment or an apology' or 'investment in underprivileged communities.'"[3] True reparations, according to the United Nations, must include (1) cessation of the harm being done and assurance that it will not be repeated, (2) restoring those harmed to their situation prior to the harm being done, (3) compensating financially those harmed for anything that cannot be fully restored, (4) satisfaction of moral injury through apology and acknowledgement, and (5) providing rehabilitation through medical, psychological, or any other care that is needed.

Achieving the goal of reparations for Black Americans will take unprecedented social pressure and government action. It will take people all over the country waking up to the reality of our nation's history and present, joining together to create a culture of repair. This book offers one hundred steps that will move us forward toward the goal.

These steps are divided into four categories, with varying levels of investment and consequence:

Individual reparations are things that individuals seeking to remove the stain of racism can do to mitigate harm done to African

Americans. These actions begin with simply acknowledging one's privilege as it relates to white supremacy and the harm done by white supremacy, educating oneself and others to resist and oppose that ideology, and providing what aid one can to those who have been adversely affected by it. The individual level is a place to start but is not enough, on its own, to repair the damage that has been done. While these actions do not remove the need for action by the government and other institutions that enacted policies which subjugated and oppressed African Americans, they do provide a course of action for individuals who are tired of waiting for their government to do what is morally right and desire to use their own initiative and resources to make this country more just for African Americans.

Societal reparations are the efforts of people in groups—connected by proximity or affiliation—to amend for past and present actions that have had a debilitating effect on African Americans. Under this approach you will see overlapping categories for more pluralistic solutions coordinated by businesses, nonprofits, community improvement groups, and more. While churches are specifically addressed in chapter 4, church groups working to improve their communities will want to consider the action steps listed in chapter 2. Under this approach, Black and non-Black communities can work together to implement community-based reparations that focus on research, redress, and restitution.

Institutional reparations are the truest and most comprehensive form of justice and accountability. This approach requires the participation of the public, governmental entities that permitted, legalized, or even mandated heinous acts for which no repair has ever been given. For justice to be done, citizens must advocate for a national movement of reparations and vote for leaders who will advance these policy initiatives. Institutional reparations would signal the beginning of a new era when healing and harmony are truly possible in this country.

Spiritual reparations include ways in which houses of faith participate in repairing the spiritual harm done to African Americans. Throughout American history, white Christians have used their faith and Scripture to justify the enslavement and abuse of African Americans—promulgating false ideas such as the claim that Black people had no souls and that our skin color was a curse from God.

From bombings of Black churches to the whitewashing of church history and Jesus himself, spiritual harm has been done and must be repaired by white Christians today.

Black Americans must be the strongest people on earth, for all we have endured; and still, we persevere. The greatest strength we can manifest is not showing how much we can push or pull. On the contrary, the hardest exhibition of strength is shown by what we can hold. An eight-ounce glass of water is easy to lift while you sip it, but how long can you hold it with arms outstretched? I often think of those strong saints who, after the 1921 Tulsa Race Massacre, did not pull out and leave, nor did they push themselves to do something different. No, they held their tenuous position, a revolutionary act of immense strength.

Rosa Parks staying in her seat on a Montgomery bus, knowing she was going against Jim Crow laws, was indeed a revolutionary act. Winston County staying in the Union when every other county in Alabama chose to secede was a revolutionary act. Blacks staying in the South after emancipation, fighting for true participation in a democracy—while local white residents tried with every tool in their arsenal, from the grandfather clause and literacy tests to poll taxes and lynchings, to keep them from voting—was a revolutionary act.

Advocacy and agitation, willingly putting the needs of a broader goal before your own personal wants, is revolutionary, and fighting for reparations is the most significant political, cultural, and spiritual revolutionary cause of our generation. Joining this most noble cause unites us with the revolutionary fighters of yesteryear. As emancipation was for Frederick Douglass and Harriet Tubman, as Black spiritual upliftment and liberation were for Bishop Henry McNeal Turner, as self-love and self-determination were for Marcus Garvey, Malcolm X, Fred Hampton, and Stokely Carmichael, as civil rights was for the Rev. Dr. Martin Luther King, John Lewis, Rosa Parks, and Fannie Lou Hamer, so should reparations be for us today.

This is their revolution. And now it's ours.

Chapter 1

Individual Reparations

One common objection to the concept of reparations is that individuals alive today did not enslave anyone nor personally implement the black codes and other racist policies. True enough; the very definition of systemic racism conveys that it is not purely the malice of individuals that prevents equality but the laws, structures, and norms of a society. Individuals acting alone cannot make or unmake unjust systems. Systemic problems require systemic solutions. So why start with individual reparations?

My faith teaches me that small acts by individuals can have a major impact on the lives of others, and even on my own soul. The same can be said for individual acts of reparation. If individuals do something, no matter how small, it can have a major impact on others, and a cumulative effect as we seek to make this world more just.

Imagine the disciples hearing Jesus speaking the words in Matthew 25:35–40:

> "'For I was hungry and you gave me food, I was thirsty and you gave me something to drink, I was a stranger and you welcomed me, I was naked and you gave me clothing, I was sick and you took care of me, I was in prison and you visited me.' Then the righteous will answer him, 'Lord, when was it that we saw you hungry and gave you food or thirsty and gave you something to drink? And when was it that we saw you a stranger and welcomed you or naked and gave you clothing?

> And when was it that we saw you sick or in prison and visited you?' And the king will answer them, 'Truly I tell you, just as you did it to one of the least of these brothers and sisters of mine, you did it to me.'"

Notice that the righteous did not say, "Well, I am not the reason you are hungry and thirsty," or "You got yourself incarcerated." No! As individuals, they worked together to find and meet those in need. Jesus is seen here identifying with the oppressed and those who are in need. Jesus also commends the righteous individuals for doing something for a particular vulnerable population, whether or not they personally participated in their oppression.

Similarly, the hero of the Good Samaritan parable sees a man lying beaten on the side of the road—a man he had not personally harmed and to whom he had no official obligation—and uses his own resources to restore the stranger to health.

> "He went to him and bandaged his wounds, treating them with oil and wine. Then he put him on his own animal, brought him to an inn, and took care of him. The next day he took out two denarii, gave them to the innkeeper, and said, 'Take care of him, and when I come back I will repay you whatever more you spend.'" (Luke 10:34–35)

When Jesus tells us to "go and do likewise" (v. 37), he compels us to follow the example of one who valued the well-being of his neighbor without assessment of guilt or innocence. The same compassion is needed today.

There are many Americans who, when confronted with a major social problem like poverty, homelessness, or underperforming schools, believe that government solutions are an overreach that unfairly burdens taxpayers. They prefer individual solutions like donating to shelters and food pantries or volunteering to help in classrooms. These are good starting points and offer a way to personally invest in one's community. Individual reparations are also excellent starting points for people who want to address the inequities that have resulted from our country's centuries-long oppression of African Americans.

Liberty and Justice for All

Individualism is at the heart of the American dream. Part of what makes the United States of America great is the belief that individuals can rise from rags to riches. With all of its problems, America is still a land of opportunity where people can rise out of their original socioeconomic class. While certain factors like race and the educational background of one's parents indicate the likelihood of such movement, the possibility of individual upward mobility is a hallmark of American capitalism. Both for our freedoms and opportunities, the United States stands as a beacon of light in a world filled with despotic regimes, economic limitations, and corruption run amok. For these reasons and more, America remains one of the most highly sought-after places to live. In large part, those who come to this great expanse in the Western Hemisphere do so because of the infinite opportunities that exist here. Fueled by popular culture, what is seen on television and heard in music, America is thought to provide each person access to the American dream. It has given much to those who immigrated here with extraordinarily little.

Sadly, Blacks in large part have not had the privilege of such upward mobility. In 1860, Blacks owned one-half of 1 percent of the nation's wealth, and in 1990 Blacks owned only 1.5 percent of the nation's wealth.[1] In a little over one hundred years of "freedom," Black Americans had an accretion of just 1 percentage point. Such astonishing figures should serve to admonish anyone thinking that opportunities in America are equally available to all citizens. Moreover, this sad fact helps disprove the notion that the end of slavery meant instant equality and opportunity, or even unfettered access to the liberties that make economic advancement possible.

Individual liberty, epitomized in the Bill of Rights, is the backbone of our democracy. Since its inception, however, these rights have not been accessed equally. Women and people of color have had to fight for equal rights every step of the way, and even when incorporated in the letter of the law, inclusion in practice is often challenged. Part of individual reparations involves people with unfettered access to freedom using their freedom to help make those whose rights have been limited more free.

Consider the ways certain rights have been denied to Black Americans. The First Amendment states, "Congress shall make no law respecting an establishment of religion, or prohibiting the free exercise thereof; or abridging the freedom of speech, or of the press; or the right of the people peaceably to assemble, and to petition the Government for a redress of grievances." The rights named in this amendment outline a rudimentary belief of what it means to be free: to worship in accordance with one's conscience, to say and write what one pleases, to gather together, and to use these freedoms to critique even the very government granting these rights. However, African Americans have not always had these rights protected.

The Black-owned *Tulsa Star* newspaper printed articles critical of racism and the white power structure and encouraged Blacks to be more politically and socially active; during the 1921 massacre, the owner of the paper was run out of town and the warehouse the newspaper was in was bombed. Football player Colin Kaepernick has not been signed by any NFL team since taking a knee during the National Anthem in 2016 to protest police brutality. In the summer of 2020, when Black Lives Matter protesters marched in Washington, DC, they were met with fierce force from police and the government. When Blacks protest, no matter how mild their expression or assembly, from taking a knee to encouraging political activism, there are often severe ramifications. Meanwhile, the predominantly white crowd that descended on the nation's capital on January 6, 2021, had the endorsement of the president and other elected officials. Many in the Republican Party continue to defend those who stormed the halls of Congress in an act of insurrection, calling it "legitimate political discourse."[2]

The action items following this chapter will explain ways to use your freedoms of speech, press, and assembly to advocate for those whose freedoms have been limited.

Consider also the Second Amendment: "A well-regulated Militia, being necessary to the security of a free State, the right of the people to keep and bear Arms, shall not be infringed."

I fully support the right of Americans to bear arms, but I cannot help but notice the discrepancy in the amount of debate and funds used to defend this right as compared to defending those outlined in the First Amendment. In too many urban communities in America it is far easier to get a gun than it is to purchase a book. No wonder deaths due to homicide continue to rise in communities of color. Meanwhile, "stand your ground" laws protect individuals who shoot and kill unarmed Blacks like Trayvon Martin, killed in 2012 by self-appointed neighborhood watchman George Zimmerman, who was acquitted.

So, in urban communities this great freedom is unfortunately used as a sword giving access to guns to people who need more books, and in suburban communities it is used a shield in defense when unarmed innocent Blacks are killed.

The Third and Fourth Amendments are intended to protect people from unwarranted invasion of their private space. The Third Amendment protects citizens from being required to house soldiers, which felt very pertinent to a country still reeling from the American Revolution, when soldiers would just take quarters in or possession of people's homes. The right to feel safe and protected in one's own space remains central to our feelings of freedom.

Aggressive and disproportionate policing in Black communities is similarly invasive, even when the letter of the law is not violated. Since the time of slave patrols, African Americans have been under surveillance and threat. Law enforcement today is not like Andy Griffith, with his innocuous badge and gun, but more like a paramilitary group, made up of many former soldiers and equipped with military-grade equipment. Overpolicing predominantly Black areas is both a cause and an effect of inaccurate perceptions of Black men, who are in many cases no more criminal than their white counterparts. For example, a disproportionate number of drug-related arrests are of Black men (more than 25 percent, when only around 14 percent of Americans are Black), even though "drug use rates do not differ substantially by race and ethnicity and drug users generally purchase drugs from people of the same race or ethnicity." Similarly, "the ACLU found that blacks were 3.7 times more likely to be arrested for marijuana possession than whites in 2010, even though their rate of marijuana usage was comparable."[3]

Today another Third Amendment is needed for Black, brown, and other groups as it relates to technology. Edward Snowden showed the world just how much the American government observed the everyday life of Americans, and we know that even as far back as the 1960s, technology has been used strategically in Black communities to monitor and stifle organizing.[4] Virtually, the government has taken quarters in our homes, cars, and offices without us ever asking them to come in. Through personal items such as cell phones, televisions, computers, and smart refrigerators, the government, not to even mention the technology companies that we utilize, has the ability to take quarters in our space.

The Fourth Amendment prohibits "unreasonable searches and seizures" and warrants issued without probable cause. While this freedom works very well for most Americans, it is too often violated when policing Black communities. Cities across America have implemented "no-knock warrants," virtually nullifying the protection of the Fourth Amendment. This is how police entered the home of Breonna Taylor, the young African American woman who was fatally shot by police in Louisville, Kentucky, in 2020. The same shameful abuse of power was used in the killing of Amir Locke in Minneapolis in 2022.

The Fifth through Eighth Amendments provide guidelines for our legal system. Most people identify the Fifth Amendment with the phrase "I plead the Fifth," referring to its prohibition against compelling anyone to "be a witness against himself." This amendment also protects citizens from being charged twice for the same crime ("double jeopardy"). Most significantly, however, the Fifth Amendment states that Americans cannot be "deprived of life, liberty, or property, without due process of law; nor shall private property be taken for public use, without just compensation." Closely related, the Sixth Amendment guarantees the right to a "speedy and public trial, by an impartial jury," with the aid of witnesses and counsel.

There is not enough paper in the world to write detailing the gross ambivalence to and outright rejection of these rights for African Americans. Whether it be in Elaine, Arkansas; Tulsa, Oklahoma; East St. Louis; Rosewood, Florida; Wilmington, North Carolina; or any other city in which terror was inflicted on citizens in response to an alleged infraction by a Black person, no due process was considered. In the case of the Tulsa Race Massacre, for instance, the white mob went to the county jail to abduct Dick Rowland and hang him because during a large part of American history, the sentiment was that the court system was too good for Blacks to go through. They thought, why waste taxpayer dollars on a trial, jury, judge, and prison, when we all know he or she is guilty, so let's just hang them. And hang them they did. According to the Equal Justice Initiative, between 1877 (the end of Reconstruction) and 1950, there were more than 4,400 racial terror lynchings in America.[5] This does not include the thousands of people who suffered when Black neighborhoods and businesses were burned to the ground, people were killed, and survivors were placed in concentration camps.[6]

Furthermore, accused Blacks who did receive a trial hardly ever saw an impartial jury, as in the case of the "Scottsboro Boys," convicted of raping two white women despite the lack of evidence. Even when Blacks were killed by whites, the partial juries were almost always sympathetic to the white defendants, as in the case of Emmett Till's killers in 1955.

These horrid occurrences of racial violence make mockery of the Fifth and Sixth Amendments. In fact, but for a few exceptions such as Rosewood, Florida, where in 1994, the nine survivors of a 1923 massacre were awarded cash payments and their descendants received cash and college scholarships, virtually none of these injustices have been repaired nor even investigated, much less was any white perpetrator brought to justice.[7] If we believe that "all men are created equal," how can one group (Blacks) suffer loss of life, property, and liberty without ever having the opportunity to seek redress in the courts? America owes them because America failed them. These Black individuals suffered violent racial attack at the hands of white individuals under the protection of law, and now it is time for both individuals and government to help repair the devastating harm that was caused.

The Seventh Amendment offers the same rights for a civil trial that the Sixth provides in criminal cases. Many situations in which Black Americans might seek reparations would be through the civil court system, and yet the most common reason civil cases are thrown out is the statute of limitations. When you consider the harm done to Black people, and the agency they held at the time of the wrongdoing, it is easy to see why those immediately impacted did not see the courts as a realistic option for their redress, in large part because racism was central to mainstream American society and white racial terror was America's favorite pastime long before baseball was invented. Furthermore, there are some things so gross, so abominable and unconscionable, like what has happened to Black people in America, that recompense should not be barred by statutes of limitations. There is no expiration date on morality. If something was terribly wrong in 1864, it is still wrong today. The passage of time does not make something less wrong, it only compounds the damage and multiplies the suffering.

The Eighth Amendment states, "Excessive bail shall not be required, nor excessive fines imposed, nor cruel and unusual punishments inflicted." The torture inflicted on lynching victims certainly qualifies as "cruel and unusual," not to mention the horrors of slavery before that, and our entire legal and penal system continues to unfairly burden Black families through excessive bail and mass incarceration.

Because of the prohibitive cost of bail and the pressure to make a plea deal to avoid the terrible experiences in American jails, 74 percent of those locked up in local jails in America have not been convicted of a crime, according to a 2020 report by the Prison Policy Initiative.[8] Doubly vexing is that bail, an instrument created to provide freedom to those charged with a crime, is now being implemented as a tool for keeping people in bondage.

The bail system has been largely taken over by for-profit insurance companies to keep people in financial hardship and at risk of being reincarcerated long after their sentence is done. According to an American Civil Liberties Union (ACLU) report, "The for-profit bail industry is responsible for $14 billion in bonds each year, collecting around $2 billion a year in profits."[9] Those profiteering off of the prison system are exploiting the poor. Due to these practices, people who have not been proven guilty of a crime are detained in jail and their families are saddled with debt even if the person was later found innocent.

America's prison-industrial complex harms people of all races, but African Americans suffer disproportionately, as researchers David Arnold, Will Dobbie, and Crystal S. Yang reported in 2018:

Racial disparities exist at every stage of the U.S. criminal justice system. Compared to observably similar whites, blacks are more likely to be searched for contraband, more likely to experience police force, more likely to be charged with a serious offense, more likely to be convicted, and more likely to be incarcerated. Racial disparities are particularly prominent in the setting of bail: in our data, black defendants are 3.6 percentage points more likely to be assigned monetary bail than white defendants and, conditional on being assigned monetary bail, receive bail amounts that are $9,923 greater.[10]

Although Blacks make up 12 percent of the US population, we make up 38 percent of the jail population in America. That is triple our number in the general population. Does that mean that Blacks are three times more criminal than other American citizens? Of course not. No, we need to critically examine policing in majority Black communities (relevant to the discussion of societal and institutional reparations later in this book), and individually we need to explore why people feel the need to call the police on Blacks for doing innocuous acts like going to work, barbecuing, and so many other mundane activities.

What those endeavoring to assist in providing individual reparations need to understand is that after emancipation from chattel slavery, the institution did not go away, it simply evolved, and this evolution was empowered by the US Constitution, in the same amendment that supposedly liberated enslaved people. The Thirteenth Amendment, passed in 1865, says, "Neither slavery nor involuntary servitude, except as a punishment for crime whereof the party shall have been duly convicted, shall exist within the United States, or any place subject to their jurisdiction."

Did you catch that? In liberating enslaved people from involuntary servitude, the Thirteenth Amendment legalized slavery as punishment for a crime. Therefore, immediately after enslaved people were freed, states and communities began to pass laws circumscribing Black life, through vagrancy laws, making it illegal to be unemployed, and through loopholes in contracts for the only jobs available for Blacks during this time in the South—sharecropping and menial labor. Convict leasing, also known as chain gangs, dominated the southern workforce in the aftermath of slavery, hired out to businesses or the state to dig ditches, work on roads, construct buildings, and fulfill other public utility functions. This is but one way that the United States has kept African Americans under the thumb of oppression for more than a century and a half beyond emancipation.

Free to Advance the Cause of Freedom

Clearly, America's moral and political transgressions have transformed its own Bill of Rights into a bill of what ought to be made right for African Americans. Hence this author calls on individuals to take action toward righting these wrongs. The individual action steps laid out in the pages that follow are a starting point. Using your own time, energy, and resources will make a difference on a small scale, empowering you to join together with others in your community to make bigger changes, and ultimately to influence government institutions to make reparations on a national level.

Those who initiate individual reparations are like those abolitionists who individually found ways to liberate enslaved people from bondage. They did not own enslaved people themselves nor did they support the idea, but they still went a step further and sought ways as individuals to dismantle the wicked institution. Author Harriet Beecher Stowe wrote antislavery novels and journalist William Lloyd Garrison chronicled the terrible deeds and abuses of slave owners. While Harriet Tubman personally led at least seventy people to freedom on the Underground Railroad, other individuals provided their homes, churches, and barns as stops to conceal weary passengers. Frederick Douglass spoke vehemently against slavery from his own experience as a former enslaved person. These individuals were all seen as radicals but acted for others because of their faith. Their individual bravery should be an inspiration to those of us who believe in true justice to do the same. You do not have to be personally participating in or directly suffering from oppression as terrible as slavery to want to eradicate and bring others relief from racial injustice.

Action 1

Acknowledge Your Privilege

The term *white privilege* entered our contemporary lexicon when women's studies professor Peggy McIntosh published a paper in 1988 called "White Privilege and Male Privilege: A Personal Account of Coming to See Correspondences through Work in Women's Studies." Her paper included forty-six examples of this privilege, holding up a mirror to white Americans' experience and opening a window into how their experiences are not normative for nonwhites, especially Black Americans. These examples include seeing people of your own race commonly represented in media, having "flesh"-colored bandages be similar in color to your own flesh, and facing a person of your own race when you see "the person in charge."[11]

The first thing an individual can do to begin repairing the injustice to Black Americans is to personally accept the truth that there exists a privilege in this country for those who have white skin. Acknowledging this privilege does not diminish any accomplishment of the acknowledger or the difficulty in overcoming challenges. It is simply a humble statement of awareness that life is easier (not easy) because of the white skin that one has.

Consider an analogy: you can walk a mile barefoot on a rocky road, but it's a lot easier to walk that same mile with socks on and a whole lot easier to walk that mile with walking shoes on. Neither article of clothing takes away the truth that you walked the mile, but it is honest and fair to acknowledge that you walked in socks or shoes and that those who walked in bare feet may need more attention paid to their bruised feet after their walk.

Another way of recognizing that privilege exists is asking yourself this question: Would I want to trade places with the person who had to walk the mile on a rocky road with no shoes or socks? Would any white person want to trade places with a Black person in light of racial profiling by police and store clerks; having a lower life expectancy and net worth; or facing discrimination in applying for a home loan, country club membership, or job?

The American colonies were founded by European immigrants

for other European immigrants. This land was never meant to be a place where anyone besides white settlers could prosper. The egalitarian populism that swept through America from the American Revolution, the land rush of the westward expansion, the establishment of public education, the New Deal, and the GI Bill were all meant to improve the lives of white Americans. That is privilege: to have a nation, from its inception, create laws, social norms, and customs to solely benefit people like you.

One way to subvert white privilege is by raising awareness of it. Hence, writing an opinion column acknowledging how you've benefited from white privilege and participation in white supremacy, or privately sharing this information with an organization that is seeking reparations and needs such anecdotal information, is a great first step that white individuals can take. The voices of white allies for reparations are invaluable in this fight to change the hearts and minds of Americans. Additionally, if you are being interviewed on a podcast or for a magazine, or if you receive an award, be up front and acknowledge your privilege. You could say something like, "I first and foremost want to acknowledge the ways my white privilege has helped get me here."

Using your voice to share that idea helps more people understand the systemic levels of white supremacy. Acknowledging one's privilege is akin to golf players acknowledging their handicap so that the game can be fairer for everyone. Privilege does not disappear when it is acknowledged, but doing so provides context for recognizing how systemically America has catered to people with white or fairer skin.

Action 2

Support Black-Owned Businesses

America had no problem utilizing Black labor when it was free or available for a slave wage. However, once Blacks went into business for themselves, providing goods and services of equal value to those of white-owned businesses, patronage subsided precipitously. Whereas Blacks frequently shop at white-owned establishments, you seldom see whites at Black-owned businesses. If the ten-to-one racial wealth gap is ever going to change, this socioeconomic dynamic should change. It is a form of reparations for individuals to intentionally patronize Black-owned businesses. If necessary, go out of your way to do this.

Free enterprise has been the catapult out of poverty for many. Unfortunately, Blacks have had to start their businesses without the assistance of a full market of clientele. Black business owners have less probability of getting affordable loans and reasonable leases and face more barriers that make starting a business even more challenging. Due to the low wealth of Black families, start-up capital is rarely available and enormous amounts of discretionary liquidity are nearly impossible to find.

During virtually every race massacre in this country, Black-owned businesses have been attacked. After the citizens of Greenwood rebuilt Black Wall Street, the construction of the interstate highway through the heart of the business district once again displaced Black-owned businesses. That same fate has met several historic places of Black enterprise. The history of state-sanctioned mob violence, codified Jim Crow, price hikes on goods used in Black stores, and pejorative stereotypes of Blacks that impede business growth make clear the unequal playing field on which Black entrepreneurs have to compete.

Seeking out Black professionals and Black-owned businesses provides a financial boost and an opportunity for increased exposure to businesses that have historically not been given access to capital to either improve or better market themselves. Being intentional about this helps expose all Americans to the richness that is Black commerce, showing everyone that quality of goods and services knows no color. In every industry there are exceptional Blacks who are waiting to bless their patrons with outstanding service. Black real estate agents, doctors, lawyers, bankers, technicians, carpenters, grocers, construction workers, fashion designers, producers, and journalists are standing ready to serve.

Individuals taking this approach are not waiting for the government to pass bills or for banks to provide loans investing in Black-owned businesses. Instead, they aim to invest in these vital businesses individually by patronizing enterprises owned by African Americans.

Action 3

Check Your DNA and Family History

Do genealogy research to discover if your family ever owned enslaved people, participated in the slave trade, or participated in one of the four thousand racial terror lynchings between 1877 and 1950. You can begin by talking with older relatives and searching public records; there are also many online tools, including some that start with DNA testing, that can help you connect with distant relatives and learn from their research into your ancestors.

White families need to know the role they played in the slave trade in the United States. The crimes against African Americans were not committed by aliens or ghosts (even though the Ku Klux Klan dressed in sheets to resemble ghosts); they were committed by real people with spouses and children and grandchildren.

If you do find out your family owned enslaved people or participated in the trade or acts of racial terror, then work to identify the families affected and pay reparations. This repair can be in the form of direct payments to descendants of enslaved people, or it could be in the form of land, especially if your family still owns the land on which enslaved people used to work. Become an "angel investor" in the businesses that the descendants of enslaved people have. Whatever you do, do not attempt to force them to forgive you or act as though they should be indebted to you for reaching out.

Whatever reparations are given individually here, they should increase the autonomy of the descendants of the enslaved people, not diminish it. Share insights your research revealed about the family of those who were enslaved. Along these same lines, paying for the DNA or genealogy research of enslaved people's descendants can be a form of individual repair, helping them find the links to their past that were robbed from them.

Kidnapping Africans from their homeland, slave traders also stripped them of their identity. Making it illegal to speak their native language, changing their names, and splitting up families by selling them far and wide, slavers aimed to sever the connection to enslaved people's ancestral tribes, culture, and homeland. After emancipation, one of the first things the enslaved people did was try to find their family members who had been sold away to various plantations. These enslaved people were mothers, fathers, sons, daughters, uncles, and aunts, and too many were never reunited.

DNA testing and genealogy research can help by giving Black Americans information about the tribes from which they are descended and connecting them with distant family members who reside in the United States. If you have the privilege of knowing your family history, use that knowledge to help repair the past for others.

Action 4

Decolonize Your Bookshelf

You are only as informed as the books you read and the news you watch. Part of the reason there is such a great ideological divide in America today is because there is no longer a shared source of information. Our political views determine what news channels we turn to, and our social media feeds end up being an echo chamber of our own beliefs. This myopic experience of the world hardens perspectives rather than challenging them. Decolonizing our sources means choosing to learn from and follow the approaches of those who were displaced and dominated by colonizing forces, broadening our views.

Given the lack of Black history taught in schools and increasing prohibitions on teaching critical race theory, it is abundantly clear that individuals will need to educate themselves and their children on the history and ongoing pervasiveness of systemic racism in this country. In order for us to improve race relations, perform reparatory justice, and ultimately have racial healing, we need to know what happened and what we need to repair and heal from.

Purchase books by Black authors or authors who write about experiences of Black life and culture, especially as it relates to racism and oppression. You can do this for your own home library and through donations to schools and public libraries to enhance their collections.

My recommendations for starting your library include *The New*

Jim Crow by Michelle Alexander, *Race Matters* by Cornel West, the article "The Case for Reparations" and book *We Were Eight Years in Power* by Ta-Nehisi Coates, *When Affirmative Action Was White* by Ira Katznelson, *Post Traumatic Slave Syndrome* by Joy DeGruy, *The Whiteness of Wealth* by Dorothy A. Brown, *The Debt* by Randall Robinson, *The Case for Black Reparations* by Boris I. Bittker, *A Raisin in the Sun* by Lorraine Hansberry, *The Bluest Eye* by Toni Morrison, *Invisible Man* by Ralph Ellison, *The 1619 Project* by Nikole Hannah-Jones, *The Love Songs of W. E. B. DuBois* by Honorée Fanonne Jeffers, *Up from Slavery* by Booker T. Washington, *The Autobiography of Malcolm X* by Alex Haley, *The Color Purple* by Alice Walker, *Why We Can't Wait* by Martin Luther King Jr., *Come Hell or High Water* by Michael Eric Dyson. I could recommend many more.

Whether fiction or nonfiction, the work of Black writers will help you to see the world through different eyes. In addition, purchasing books by Black authors and from Black-owned bookstores financially supports people who have historically had opportunities limited. Without decolonizing your bookshelf, it will be difficult to decolonize your mind from the shackles of neo-imperialism and white supremacy.

Action 5

Think before Calling the Police

Most interactions with police do not result in death. But when they do, Black people have a higher chance of being the victims. Blacks are twice as likely as whites to be fatally shot by a police officer.[12] Individual reparations can include becoming aware of the potential for racial profiling and police violence against unarmed Black people and practicing greater discretion when considering whether police need to be called.

Be aware of the tendency for white people to call the police on Black people who are exhibiting innocuous behavior in predominantly white spaces, where these white individuals feel that Blacks do not belong. Black people have had cops called on them for playing music during a backyard barbecue, birdwatching in Central Park, and sitting down before ordering in a Starbucks. Ask yourself if anything truly illegal or dangerous is happening that would necessitate the involvement of law enforcement. Learn who your neighbors are so that you do not make assumptions about them, and if you notice that the Black resident is not active in the neighborhood, personally seek them out and encourage their participation.

The fear of Black people is real, and the gross mischaracterization of Black people as violent, thuggish, disposable, and criminal has led to too many Black people killed by police or by citizens who illogically feel threatened. Individuals can play a greater role in not being so paranoid at the presence of Blacks in their midst.

Action 6

Visit Places of Historical Note

Reading a book or watching a movie on race and the role it plays is one method of seeing the picture of four hundred years of oppression. It is an entirely different thing when you can go and see the monstrosity of what happened where it happened.

Being from the historic city of Tuskegee, Alabama, I gained a wealth of knowledge that I could never have gotten from a book. I was born in John Andrew Hospital, where the Tuskegee Syphilis Study was conducted; I saw the buildings in which Booker T. Washington founded what is now Tuskegee University; I lived a few minutes from Moton Field, where the Tuskegee Airmen learned to fly; I passed Lionel Richie's home every day going to school; and I saw the instruments used by George Washington Carver in his laboratory.

Seeing historic places firsthand helps us better understand their context, significance, and what life was like for the people involved in events there. It immerses you into history so that you can notice the details and feel the weight of others' experiences, especially in places where gross acts against humanity were done.

Travel part of the Civil Rights Trail, which includes sites in fifteen states and the District of Columbia. Visit the docks where enslaved people were sold, sites of massacres like Tulsa, famous churches, and the homes of Black leaders. After decades of being falsely romanticized, many plantations are now telling the truth about the atrocities committed there.

Additionally, visiting these places of historical note can improve the economy of the communities you visit, which are typically overwhelmingly Black.

Action 7

Write Op-Eds and Post on Social Media

Many individual acts of reparation require some sort of financial investment, even as small as driving farther to patronize a Black-owned business. This action requires nothing but internet access, available free in public libraries if you do not have service in your home.

Allies in the cause of racial justice can use their First Amendment right of free speech to share their opinion in support of reparations. Before the emergence of social media, writing letters to the newspaper was a common way for ordinary people to have their voices heard in the public sphere. This is even easier now that you can submit letters to the editor online for potential print and digital posting. Less formally, you can share your support for reparations on social media platforms. Whether in a 500-word op-ed or a 280-character tweet, simply express what you find to be the most convincing arguments for reparations, plus a single, small action readers can take in response.

For those who do not like to write, post a video of yourself making this argument. Even adding the hashtag #reparationsnow at the end of every post can send a message to those you connect with online. Whatever platform you have, use it to call attention to and advocate justice for those who have suffered the brunt of racism in this country.

The collective force of individuals throughout the country sharing #reparationsnow on social media and filling the in-boxes of

every major newspaper in America with opinion pieces supporting reparations could have a world-changing impact.

Action 8

Run for Office

Probably one of the most selfless acts of individual reparations is
to offer yourself for public service. Serving others by holding elec-
tive office is one of the most noble sacrifices a person can make.
The reparations movement does not have enough candidates who
publicly campaign for office in support of this issue. Reparations
is seen as too toxic to run on. Therefore, as with most toxic issues,
campaign consultants (who may not be for reparations themselves)
advise candidates to keep quiet until they get elected.

We need individuals willing to run for office advocating for reparations, true justice that has been denied for far too long. The benefits are twofold: their candidacy helps push the topic of reparations
to the forefront of the discussion, challenging other candidates to
respond and voters to consider the issue; and second, if they win,
they will be able to push for reparation plans that are long overdue.

Reparations should not be a partisan issue. Historically it has
not been. Republican President Ronald Reagan and a Republican-
led Congress approved a reparations package for Japanese Americans for their treatment during World War II. Both parties have
supported reparations for Jewish Americans in response to the
Holocaust and continued aid to Native Americans. There is prec-
edent for future candidates from both parties running on a pro-
reparations platform, unless one of those parties has something
against Black people.

Ever since 1989, Democrats have introduced House Bill 40 to
establish the Commission to Study and Develop Reparation Pro-
posals for African Americans, and thus far the only supporters of
House Bill 40 are Democrats. It is a sad state of affairs when every
other reparations proposal has had bipartisan support except reparations for Black suffering. That is why it is important to urge candidates from either party to make reparations a central issue in their

campaign, encourage people of goodwill to run for office, and consider being that person yourself.

Be it city councillor, county commissioner, state representative, member of Congress, governor, senator, or president, the reparations movement needs individuals who are willing to campaign on the issue of reparations and bring America's systemic problem of racism and its lack of remedy back into the political discourse and mainstream conversation. More than that, we need people in government who will implement solutions.

Action 9

Host Conversation Parties

Social influencers, campaign bundlers, and church planters have found there is something greatly beneficial about hosting a gathering at their home. It brings a level of trust and transparency that other venues cannot. The intimate setting of a house is a poignantly safe space to deliberate and discuss important topics. Casual conversations are the best tool to help convince people of a hard truth, and reparations is as controversial and complex as issues come in the American political discourse.

While you may not be able to accommodate a large gathering, the small group of those with whom you have a relationship will feel significant and safe, sharing and asking productive and sometimes controversial questions because they are not in front of a massive crowd of people. For these reasons and more, individuals hosting house parties can be pivotal in moving the reparations conversation forward.

When discussing sensitive subject matter, there is a great need for trust and candor. Careful listening and creative problem solving are key components of a rich conversation about both the virtues and challenges of reparations.

To plan such a gathering, follow these steps:

1. First, create an invitation list. Choose people who are open-minded and thoughtful, willing to engage in conversation without dominating or shutting down others.

2. Choose reading materials for the attendees. An article like Ta-Nehisi Coates's "The Case for Reparations" is a good choice for an initial gathering. If there is enough time and you are confident all of your attendees can afford the purchase (or have someone sponsor them), you can choose a book that teaches the history and complexity of the issue and provides options and ways to implement them.

3. Select a facilitator. It doesn't have to be you! Preferably this will be someone well versed in deliberative forums and the topic. Having served as a facilitator, I can say with certainty that retaining one's impartiality and objectivity is essential for those who seek to be a facilitator, as is the ability to direct a conversation to keep the group on topic and prevent one or two people from dominating the discussion.

4. Issue your invitations with a clear explanation of what the gathering will entail, what materials to read in advance, and what to expect during the conversation.

5. Plan your food options, refreshments, or a meal.

6. Keep notes during the event and build on them for future meetings with either the same or a different group. These meetings can take place once a quarter or as often as you desire.

Action 10

Become an Affiliate Member
of Predominantly Black Organizations

Due to the historical significance of Black organizations in our country and the role they have played in developing leaders, mentoring children, registering voters, submitting information, and warehousing photographs and memorabilia and more, we need to make sure that we keep them alive.

As the nation's oldest civil rights organization, the National Association for the Advancement of Colored People helped fight for school integration and challenged racist policies, from segregation to voting restrictions. The NAACP was so successful it was banned in several southern states, prohibiting it from soliciting members, receiving dues, or raising money. Alabama and other states tried to squeeze it out of existence. Meanwhile, overtly racist organizations such as the Ku Klux Klan and White Citizens' Councils were able to operate with impunity and had no fear of reprisal. In fact, for much of the 1900s, in order to be elected to any position of power, individuals seeking office had to at least appeal to and in most cases be a member of both.

Organizations like the NAACP, Urban League, Rainbow PUSH Coalition, Southern Christian Leadership Conference, Repairers of the Breach, National Action Network, and Black Lives Matter are critical in leading the fight for social justice and reparations, advocacy, voter registration, and education, and supporting them can be a monumental part of reparations. This action increases the viability and diversity of Black organizations in America, with new members and sponsors seeking not to control the organizations but to identify with and support them so that they can do what they feel is needed. Becoming a dues-paying member or affiliate of one or more predominantly Black organizations is a dynamic form of repair without which some organizations might cease to exist in the coming decades.

Action 11

Provide Bail Assistance

According to the Justice Policy Institute, in 2006 average bail was about $55,000. That was more than the annual pay of about 82 percent of US wage earners. In the same year, bail bondsmen were paid more than $1.4 billion across the country.[13]

I will not begin a homily against the cash bail system and how terrible this for-profit enterprise is for our justice system, to the point of undermining our Constitution. (That treatise will come in chap. 3.) Instead, let's focus on what individuals can do to help Black families caught up in bail debt. First off, it needs to be stated that just because someone is in debt to a bail bondsman does not mean they are a criminal. Bail is paid whether you are innocent or not, and if yours is paid by a bail bondsman (which is not uncommon, because most Americans do not have $55,000 lying around), then the customer must pay that back. And if you are released before the bond is paid, in some cases you can go back to jail for not paying.

This system is particularly unjust for Black Americans because ever since the end of chattel slavery there has been an all-out assault on Blacks to incarcerate them for any and every thing. The Thirteenth Amendment itself, as we discussed, leaves the door open for slavery "as a punishment for crime," so incarceration became a way to maintain access to unpaid labor. Later, when the prison system became privatized, incarceration became even more profitable for those in power.

This action encourages individuals to pay the bail bond of an accused person and, if that bond is already in collections, assist them with the payments. Do this by identifying and contacting Blacks who have been booked and must post bail, or donate to organizations such as the Bail Project, which pays bail for people in need. Just ensure that your support goes to an African American person to offset the damaging financial effects of the overpolicing of Black communities.

Action 12

Sponsor Phone Calls between a Child and Their Incarcerated Parent

While action 11 deals with the financial harm the penal system inflicts on Blacks, this action addresses an emotional harm of mass incarceration. Communication between children and their parents is the most important social behavior we have. The life lessons, admonishments, and commendations from parents have a prescriptive and fulfilling role in the life of children.

According to the *Washington Post*, one in nine Black children has had a parent who was incarcerated.[14] A fifteen-minute phone call from prison, on average, costs $5.74, and some prisons charge a dollar or more for each minute.[15] By partnering with agencies such as Prison Fellowship's Angel Tree and Building Families Together, or anecdotally through churches, schools, and social services, we can identify Black children whose parents are incarcerated and provide funds to cover those phone calls.

It is vital that we understand how the penal system has caused generational harm to Black Americans in numerous ways, not least of which is the debilitating effect mass incarceration has had on children. Children with no connection to their parents miss invaluable knowledge about themselves and the world. These children should not be deprived of that opportunity simply because their parents are incarcerated.

Action 13

Vote

The most significant thing an individual can do for the cause of reparations in the United States is to vote for leaders who make racial justice a priority. All of the government actions in chapter 3 depend on the elected representatives and political appointees in each government agency.

Voting is an act of supreme importance in democratic governments. In the United States, who can vote today is vastly different than it was originally. Because Blacks have been denied the right to vote or used to enlarge the voting power of others (the Three-Fifths Compromise in 1787 counted enslaved persons for the purpose of southern representation in Congress; today inmates are likewise counted as part of the population even though they cannot vote), everyone should see it is as their most noble civic duty to participate in the enfranchisement of voting. Your vote should be cast for those who aim to make America a more perfect union where there truly is liberty and justice for all.

Chapter 2

Societal Reparations

Society is defined as people living and interacting in groups, united by some common cause, culture, or proximity. Think neighborhood associations, community groups, social clubs, nonprofit organizations, for-profit companies, and even the loose affiliation of people who share certain values, political views, or priorities.

Society's role in both historic discrimination and the repair thereof involves people working together, combining their influence, to implement or challenge norms and behaviors *without the rule of law* that institutions provide. The line between societal and institutional actions can be fuzzy, however, because societal norms often end up codified into law, and laws are often ignored if societal acceptance of a practice is powerful enough. For example, exclusion of African Americans from white businesses was practiced and valued to the point that segregation became law. Lynching, on the other hand, is by definition an extrajudicial execution, but white society accepted and encouraged the practice to the point that businesses closed early so that people could go watch, entrepreneurs could sell images of the spectacle as postcards, and members of the crowd could participate in the torture, snatching up body parts as keepsakes—while law enforcement declined to intervene.

For the purposes of this book, *society* and *societal reparations* refer to actions of people working together in some form of organization. Society sanctioned slavery and watched as Black bodies were sold on the auction block. Long after the enslaved people were emancipated, white society kept the system of racial superiority in place through Jim Crow segregation, lynching, and mass incarceration. It was society that created race in the first place—a social construct, which America codified into law.

The pseudoscientific genesis for the concept of race began with Johann Friedrich Blumenbach, a German physician and anthropologist. He is considered to be one of the founders of modern zoology and anthropology. In 1790 his *Decas collectionis suae craniorum diversarum gentium illustrata* was published in Göttingen, Germany. Written in Latin, it was the first work that used measurements of the human skull to divide humanity into five groups or "races" of people: the first and most important, the Caucasian or white race from Europe; the Mongolian, yellow race, from East Asia; the Malayan, brown race, which included South Asians and Pacific Islanders; the American or red race; and the Ethiopian or black race, from sub-Saharan Africa.

Blumenbach held that whites were the first humans, that life started with them in Asia, and that everyone else came about as a degeneration of the original white race. We know now that human life began in Africa, hence the first Homo sapiens were African. Blumenbach did not support slavery, but his theory was used by others to justify the enormously profitable trade with claims of scientific evidence of white supremacy.[1] Later scientists, such as American physician Samuel George Morton, expanded the theory so far as to justify polygenism, the blasphemous notion that God had a separate creation event for each race of people. Such an idea helped promulgate the notion that Blacks and whites are not only different races but also different species.

Bringing God into the equation is how scientific racism becomes theological racism, which will be elaborated on in chapter 4. Suffice it to say for now that theological racism is the belief that God ordained Blacks to be servants and whites to be their rulers. With such false science and false theology, the social construct of race and racial difference became unquestioned fact in the United States, until nearly every aspect of society was marked by racial stratification.

The Wages of Whiteness

White American society made Blackness something to be looked down on and whiteness an attribute to be admired. W. E. B. DuBois began naming and assessing racialized capitalism and its primary beneficiaries in his 1935 work *Black Reconstruction in America*. In it DuBois argues that whiteness served as a "public and psychological wage," providing poor whites in the nineteenth and early twentieth centuries a valuable social status bound to their categorization as not Black. Hence white Americans, no matter how poor or downtrodden they might personally be, found comfort in the assurance that they were not Black.[2]

In the early days of slavery, poor whites and poor Blacks were allies. Some poor whites were indentured servants, often beaten, raped, bought, and sold in similar fashion to African enslaved people. Indigenous Americans and Blacks also joined forces in early colonial America, in part because they both recognized the avarice and vitriol of rich white men and its debilitating effect on the poor. Black and white servants joined forces against elite whites in Bacon's Rebellion of 1676, after which power brokers began to realize the potential threat of a unified underclass. In 1705, the Virginia Slave Codes made distinctions clearer by codifying limitations on the terms of indentured servitude and harsher restrictions on enslaved persons, including barring enslaved people from traveling without permission or carrying weapons, and explicitly allowing slave owners to punish enslaved people, even to the point of death, with impunity. These distinctions, as well as prohibitions against marriage and sexual relationships between the two classes, aimed to erect a social boundary that even the poorest whites would find benefit in observing.

After slavery was outlawed and Black Americans were free to relocate and engage in commerce and politics, whiteness lost its legal benefits but grew in social value, inflated to the great "psychological wage" of which DuBois wrote. White supremacy grew during the years of Reconstruction, following the Civil War, fomenting a rage that demanded enforcement of racial separation.

After being upheld by the *Plessy v. Ferguson* "separate but equal"

Supreme Court ruling in 1896, segregation once again legally reinforced the tangible benefits of white skin. Society enforced the social norms of whites-only pools, fountains, schools, cemeteries, churches, social clubs, nightclubs, places of employment, neighborhoods, and so on. Virtually all sections of white life were entirely segregated. Meanwhile, whites were free to move in and out of Black society as they wished. Blacks did not prevent whites from patronizing their businesses or attending their churches or schools. There was no punishment from Blacks for whites who wanted to enter Black-owned establishments. But white society threatened racial terror against any Black person who dared violate the social norms of Jim Crow. Ultimately if Blacks were not entering to serve whites, they were not allowed in white establishments without the risk of being killed.

The benefits of this "public and psychological wage" were not only social but also financial. Whites decry any talk of economic reparations or even welfare as "handouts," while ignoring the multiple benefits and public payments that have been given to white people throughout US history while being denied to Blacks. America took land from Native Americans and gave it to white settlers in the eighteenth and nineteenth centuries, while the "forty acres and a mule" that America promised to freed enslaved people during Reconstruction never materialized. White soldiers received benefits from the GI Bill that Black soldiers did not. Segregated white schools received necessary maintenance and new materials, while deteriorating Black schools received the old, torn books that the white schools no longer needed. Even in recent decades, America subsidized white farmers with grants and low-interest loans while denying those benefits to Black farmers.[3]

The benefits of being white in the United States are so clear and quantifiable that sociologists, historians, and the like began naming the concept as "white privilege." When the term became popularized in the 2010s, it struck a nerve in white America, and it continues to do so. Conservative commentators (as well as ordinary folk) lament the accreditation of their success to anything but their own grit and hard work, and white people get more angry about being told they have privilege than they do about the fact that others have been unfairly disadvantaged for centuries. In 2018, Robin

DiAngelo put a name to this backlash or "whitelash" to critiques of white behavior; she succinctly calls the sensitivity white America feels when discussing racism and the benefits gained due to white supremacy "white fragility."[4] Just as the naming of white privilege was met with a chorus of boos from those who held tightly to the great white lie that America does not show preferential treatment to people of white skin at the expense of everyone else, especially Blacks, the phrase "white fragility" was equally offensive.

Now, some in white America are so fragile that they want to outlaw even the teaching of anything that might be perceived as critical of the US history of race. Where once governors like George Wallace in my home state of Alabama stood in the schoolhouse door to prevent Black children from entering and learning alongside white children, now governors and legislators fight to keep schoolchildren of all races from learning that it ever happened.

Under the guise of protecting children's innocence, state legislatures throughout the country have proposed and passed laws banning books and curricula that might offend white children or lead them to believe that their ancestors were racist. No such concern was rendered for indigenous children, who were placed in 350 boarding schools and indoctrinated to believe their culture was "savage" and less valuable than that of Europeans. Nor was there any concern for the Black children all over the South who encountered angry mobs of whites as they were seeking to integrate the public schools of America. To anyone who would hold that it is not right to expose the innocent minds of children to the evils of racism, my rejoinder is: If Black and brown children are old enough to experience racism, then white children should be considered old enough to learn about it. There has never been an age requirement for Blacks to experience racism. Children were sold as enslaved people, separated from families, assaulted for going to public schools, and even gunned down by fearful adults, as Trayvon Martin was while walking home with a bag of Skittles and as Tamir Rice was while holding a toy gun at a park.

Fear and fragility are stoked in social contexts where white people insist that racism is a thing of the past and encourage one another in a mass delusion that says Black people are the crazy ones for not simply "getting over it." As white southern author William

Faulkner wrote, "The past is never dead. It's not even past." Right here in our present, we see monuments commemorating Confederate soldiers who fought and died to keep our ancestors enslaved. We pass public buildings named for those whose wealth and power were built with opportunities denied to their Black contemporaries. Our children attend schools where race-blind practices continue to privilege suburban white children over their Black peers. We jog through parks where lynchings and mass graves haunt us with deaths that still go unacknowledged.

These kinds of local homages to and echoes of our racist past remain because people allow them to, because society simply accepts them—and they can be changed when there is enough social pressure to make them unacceptable.

Making Things Right Together

In Jesus' time, an injustice that many people simply accepted was the Roman Empire's exploitative taxation system. Authorities empowered local tax collectors to gather funds from their neighbors on Rome's behalf; whatever they could gather on top of the taxes owed, they could keep as payment. Zacchaeus was one such tax collector, who got rich by cheating his fellow Jews in the Roman-occupied city of Jericho. Jesus caused quite a stir by inviting himself to Zacchaeus's house.

> All who saw it began to grumble and said, "He has gone to be the guest of one who is a sinner." Zacchaeus stood there and said to the Lord, "Look, half of my possessions, Lord, I will give to the poor, and if I have defrauded anyone of anything, I will pay back four times as much." Then Jesus said to him, "Today salvation has come to this house, because he, too, is a son of Abraham. For the Son of Man came to seek out and to save the lost." (Luke 19:7–10)

Something about Jesus' presence helped Zacchaeus recognize his wrongdoing, and with that understanding came a sense of responsibility to restore what he had stolen. Perhaps he couldn't change the whole system, but he took action to repair the injustice in his community, first by directing resources to those most in need and then by properly compensating those he had defrauded. (According to the law stated in Exod. 22:1, thieves are to repay four or five times what they stole.) This transformation was so remarkable, thus Jesus declared that salvation had come to Zacchaeus's house because of his reparative act.

We may not be individually guilty of the sin of racism, but we do participate in a society shaped by racism—and if we are white, we likely benefit from that unjust culture. Acknowledging that fact is a first step, and taking action to repair past harms and end ongoing harms can be transformative.

Societal reparations involve organizations of people seeking to atone for their past and present actions that have had a debilitating effect on African Americans. In this chapter's action steps, you will see how America's racist history leaves its mark on our neighborhoods, schools, and civic life and how you can replace that culture of racism with a culture of repair.

People who take action with this approach remind me of organizations formed during slavery, such as the American Colonization Society, started by William Lloyd Garrison, and the Free African Society, begun by Bishop Richard Allen and Absalom Jones. Both organizations not only advocated for liberation from slavery but also engaged in significant, substantive efforts to ameliorate its effects. Purchasing enslaved people to liberate them in Africa was one of the primary goals of the American Colonization Society, while assisting freed enslaved people and families was one of the goals of the Free African Society. Remnants of it are still alive today in the African Methodist Episcopal Church, the oldest predominantly Black Protestant denomination in the world.

Ordinary people have great power when they work together. They can use that social power to stoke fear and oppress others— or they can bravely collaborate to make positive change and correct the mistakes of the past.

Action 14

Remove Racially Restrictive Covenants

Far too many people live in communities where homeowners association (HOA) covenants still contain language that explicitly states that Black people (and often people of other races and particular religions as well) are not allowed to buy, lease, or occupy a house within the neighborhood. These restrictive covenants were voted on when the homeowners associations were first formed in neighborhoods across America, during the decades when discriminatory lending practices also made it financially difficult for Black families to purchase a home in predominantly white areas. Limiting opportunities for homeownership not only stymied the stability and success of Black Americans but also had a long-range financial impact, as home equity is key to creating generational wealth.

While these covenants are unenforceable, and often ignored, today, they represent what would be the rule of the day were it not for *Shelley v. Kraemer*, in which the US Supreme Court ruled them unenforceable in 1948, and for the federal Fair Housing Act of 1968. Sadly, in the hopes that one day that act will be repealed, or simply out of ignorance or lack of concern, the racist language has been left in many of these covenants, which are included in every mortgage for homes at those addresses. Black homeowners should not have to sign documents that degrade and dehumanize them. Documents that say Blacks cannot lease or purchase homes in certain neighborhoods are vestiges of a past that need to be eliminated.

Homeowners who live in houses or neighborhoods that were established before 1968 should read the fine print of their mortgages, HOA covenants, and deeds to identify racist language for removal. Actions broaden from individual to societal as homeowners inform their neighbors of this ugly history, write letters to the neighborhood association, and create a petition with which to approach the county clerk or records office. A sample letter could read: "We the undersigned do hereby declare that we would like to remove the racist language from our covenant which restricts land ownership in this neighborhood from Black people. We abhor and reject this language and want it stricken from our covenants, deeds, and mortgage documents."

The legal process for making this change official can be "arduous, if not impossible," as one *New York Times* article put it. As a result, some states are beginning to "pass laws that streamline the process." At least thirteen states did so between 2018 and early 2022.[5] If your state is not one of them, contact your legislators and work to make it so. It is beyond time to let racist bylaws be bygone.

Action 15

Rename Streets, Schools, and Buildings

When the South was soundly defeated in the Civil War, its collective psyche took a brutal blow. During the years of Reconstruction that followed, charges were filed against former Confederate soldiers and generals and later dismissed by Confederate apologist President Andrew Johnson. These newly pardoned individuals did not vanish into obscurity, but over time they developed a myth that has come to be known as the Lost Cause, defending and glorifying the Confederacy and repainting its history as heroic and just, rather than as a traitorous rebellion against the US government.

In service of this lie, all throughout the South communities began to name streets, schools, hospitals, banks, churches, cities, and counties after Confederate generals and other people who owned enslaved people and fought against the United States during the Civil War. In southern states from Virginia to Texas, you'll find places with names like Lee County, Stonewall Avenue, Jefferson Davis High School, Forrest City.

Surprisingly, many of these homages were made not in the years immediately following the Civil War, but decades later, as a backlash to Reconstruction, and in another wave during the civil rights era. Similarly, a significant number of the school names honoring the Confederacy were bestowed after the *Brown v. Board of Education* desegregation ruling in 1954. It was the society's protest of forced desegregation.

Supporters of racial justice should find it reprehensible to live in a county or city or on a street named in honor of those persons. Societies reflect what they believe in by what they allow. Honoring individuals who supported owning people and who killed American soldiers should be abominable in this country. In Germany, you will not find a public school called Hitler or a street named Goebbels, so why in America do we celebrate those who sought to keep people in bondage and sold their bodies as chattel and killed American soldiers for the states' rights to do the same? If America truly condemns the racist and horrific actions of the past, especially those involving slavery, then we must rename those elements of our society honoring generals of the Confederacy. You cannot say we as a nation abhor slavery and then allow schools, streets, and buildings to retain the names of people who participated in slavery and fought to uphold it.

Some schools, such as my alma mater, the University of Alabama, have begun changing building names that honor racists. These efforts begin through awareness campaigns informing students and faculty (or the community, in the case of streets or public buildings) of the history reflected by the name, then securing acknowledgment by those in power through written communication or a public forum and making plans to address the situation. New names may be submitted for discussion, and if the name is changed, a statement should be made explaining why the former name did not match with the values and vision of the school or community. If it is decided that the old name will be kept, a full, detailed history with condemnation of the person or incident honored in the name should be posted in a public place next to the building name (most places have simply changed the names). If done respectfully and appropriately, this process can be a healing experience for the community or school.

Action 16

Remove Confederate Memorials and Monuments

In addition to the streets, buildings, schools, counties, and cities named in honor of Confederate generals and soldiers, more than seven hundred Confederate monuments existed in the United States of America in January 2022, according to the Southern Poverty Law Center.[6]

There is one in my hometown, Tuskegee, which has an over-whelmingly Black population. It is one of the more than 122 monuments in public spaces in the state of Alabama.[7] However, the South is not the only place where these monuments are: thirty-one states have at least one, even though only eleven states were part of the Confederacy.[8]

Many of these statues were erected between 1900 and 1920, around the fiftieth anniversary of the Civil War, and later around the time of the war's hundredth anniversary as a protest of the civil rights movement, which saw great advances for Black people. Their erection was a symbol that times still had not changed that much and a reminder to the Black inhabitants of the history of the place where they dwell.

Many of these statues and monuments are in cemeteries created and maintained with public tax dollars. In my home state of Alabama, the state used tax dollars to pay for the pensions of Confederate veterans, and after their deaths, money went to support the cemeteries where the soldiers were buried and to establish a Confederate memorial. To this day, the Confederate Memorial Park receives public tax dollars. According to the *Washington Post*, in 2020—during the height of the COVID pandemic—$670,000 was spent to keep up that memorial. Meanwhile, the descendants of the enslaved people those Confederate soldiers fought to keep have not received a dime.[9]

In this action step, advocates will work to remove Confederate monuments from public grounds and to end public funding of these memorials. Social organizations can advocate for ending state-sanctioned support of Confederate memorials and monuments. Supporters of this action are patriots who love the United States of America and denounce the Confederate states as a treasonous entity that was soundly defeated by a far superior military and government. In the spirit of loving this country and pledging to defend it against all enemies, both foreign and domestic, honoring a defeated enemy dishonors all the brave men and women who have fought for this country.

Since 2015, the year a white supremacist killed nine individuals in a church in Charleston, South Carolina, momentum has been building to remove Confederate monuments. Indignation was further fueled by the racist and deadly Unite the Right rally in Charlottesville, Virginia, in 2017, and George Floyd's murder by police in 2020. More than 140 monuments have been removed from public space since 2015.[10] Unfortunately, positive movement causes some states to double down: the Alabama state legislature passed a bill in 2017 that forbids cities and counties to remove or alter a monument on public grounds that has been there more than forty years. Violators can be fined $25,000. In 2022 there was an attempt to make the bill stronger and charge cities $5,000 for each day the monument is not in its original location.[11]

It takes the energy and social capital of many people to combat legislation like this and to sway public opinion to make removing these racist monuments a clear choice. Moreover, proponents of this initiative should seek to reallocate the funds used to maintain these Confederate monuments and memorials to begin a reparations fund that will go to maintaining and improving the city or state's historic Black sites instead.

Action 17

Excavate Mass Graves

There have been more than sixty mass killings of Blacks in this country. They have occurred in every geographic area of the United States of America. Those in Tulsa, Wilmington, and Rosewood have received much coverage. But tens of thousands of African Americans have been castrated, maimed, and lynched by angry, virulent white mobs. To hide evidence of their racial terror, the killers and their accomplices put many of these bodies in mass graves.

These graves range in size but have a few things in common: typically they are near bridges, waterways, or railroads, places where land is easily permeable. Their exact locations were not officially documented by the legal authorities, but the local townspeople, especially the Black community, knew and never forgot. Sadly, the Black community was intimidated into silence, and local law enforcement never did any real investigation.

Today, bodies are still lying in mass graves all across America—individuals who have never had a proper funeral where they were committed to the ground with the words "ashes to ashes, dust to dust."

This action calls for organizations throughout the country, especially those in cities where known race massacres took place, to urge their cities to excavate all the sites where mass graves might be. Universities often have the skilled personnel to perform the excavations, while nonprofits have the means. In Tulsa, the University of Oklahoma led the research and the city of Tulsa is paying for it. But it took a community town hall meeting at Morning Star Missionary Baptist Church for me to ask the mayor of Tulsa the question about reparations and excavations. He agreed to the excavation but did not respond to the reparations part of the question.

Community and faith-based organizations can play a crucial role in creating encounters with change agents where transformation can occur, where constituents can hold elected officials accountable as we continue to pursue justice on behalf of those innocent Blacks who were killed in acts of racial terror.

Action 18

Form Local Preservation Societies

Local preservation societies can help to restore landmarks such as churches, schools, homes, and burial grounds within or for the Black community. Some historic and long-abandoned landmarks for African Americans remain, while others have been torn down for reasons including, but not limited to, blight and economic development. For generations, Blacks have been denied access to capital to build, and when they did acquire that capital, the property was undervalued, and the low appraisals reduced equity that could be used to renovate. As a result, too many historic Black landmarks are disappearing.

With this action, the community can work together through historical societies, nonprofits, and concerned citizens to restore historic Black landmarks. This could be done by applying for preservation grants and collaborating with the United Way, Habitat for Humanity, church groups, or foundations. It is important that these landmarks be repaired, remain in Black hands, and tell the history of a resilient people.

This rich American history should not be lost forever. To prevent this loss in places where the buildings are no longer there, plaques should be erected in their place, with permission from the city or local governing body. The people who lived, worked, worshiped, and were buried in those locations suffered from slavery, Jim Crow, and segregation, never seeing reparations. It would be fitting that at least the places they frequented, such as schools, churches, and burial grounds, be kept for decades to come.

Action 19

Fund Black Art Galleries or Exhibits

Art depicting Black people and culture has in large part been produced against the will of Black people, such as white artists' sculptures and paintings depicting enslaved people or pictures of lynchings that were sold and distributed as postcards. Later, minstrel shows where white performers paraded in blackface evolved into the imagery of Blacks in film, with white actors' depictions of foolish characters such as Jim Crow used to justify the "separate but equal" policy. Today, some record labels and film production studios still aim to present degrading caricatures of Black life.

To repair the harm society has inflicted on Black people through art, communities should establish Black art centers in every county of more than twenty thousand people where the Black population exceeds 30 percent. In these Black art centers, local and national Black artists, poets, musicians, and actors can display their talent. The exposure and expression of these Black artists in so many places across America would drastically change the artistic landscape in the Western Hemisphere. Never before has there been an investment such as this in the talents and artistic expressions of Black people.

This action calls for organizations to donate space to display visual art and host performing artists. It calls on nonprofits and civic organizations, especially those whose focus is the arts, to create funds to identify and support artists in their area. This investment can also assist poorly funded schools that in recent decades have had to eliminate art programs, making it less likely that Black children have structured arts lessons that could refine their skills and have the opportunity to perform and to learn from peers and professionals.

Public space to highlight Black art and Black artists in all its mediums is a way to fill the gap in schools' budget for art programs and provide children with more positive images of themselves and their community.

Action 20

Stop Appropriating Black Culture

Historical and contemporary American Black culture, in large part, is birthed out of pain, oppression, and resilience. Therefore, it is both disingenuous and insulting for others—in particular those who have profited off those exploitive racist systems and practices—to now profit from Black culture and (adding further insult to injury) to not give credit to those Blacks who originated it. This is cultural appropriation, defined by the *Oxford English Dictionary* as "the unacknowledged or inappropriate adoption of the practices, customs, or aesthetics of one social or ethnic group by members of another (typically dominant) community or society."[12] It is often committed by individuals, as in the case of Halloween costumes based on a stereotype of another culture, but is most malicious when committed commercially.

Appropriation is part of a more complex story that goes beyond mere imitation. It starts with white society's condemnation of Black styles and characteristics, then grows to whites' mockery of Blackness, and then it goes to whites' society taking those acts, habits, or creations as its own. Examples of cultural appropriation include white adoption of Black music, language, and hairstyles; skin darkening; body enhancements; and misrepresentation of Black historical persons or their inventions. They took the form of minstrel shows in the late nineteenth and early twentieth centuries, with white actors donning blackface and caricaturing Black people. The Aunt Jemima character, used to sell pancake mix, originated in a minstrel show before Nancy Green—who was born enslaved and worked for a white family most of her life—became the food company's paid spokeswoman in 1890, dressed in a mammy costume.[13] As with the Uncle Ben rice brand, white-run companies appropriate comforting, subservient images of Black people to sell their products.

White people get paid to mimic Blacks while Blacks are mocked, assaulted, or even killed for those same features. For example, Black women are discouraged from wearing braids in the workplace, especially if they work in media, appearing on television. It's a statement for us, but it's a phase for whites who move in and out of Black culture without having to pay the price of living in America as a Black person. Consider how Oprah Winfrey was critiqued for wearing thick, curly hair at her first TV news job, in the same era when Bo Derek was considered a sex symbol for appearing in cornrows and braids.[14]

This action calls for society to properly appreciate Black culture by not claiming behaviors, practices, and styles that they know they did not create. Cease aiming to monetize Black culture at the expense and exploitation of Black people. Cultural appropriation is actually theft. Consider the billions of dollars in profit made by the whiskey brand Jack Daniels. The company history claims that Jack Daniel was taught his distilling technique by a preacher; in reality, it was the expertise of Nearest Green, a man enslaved by the preacher.[15] In today's world, where trending videos on social media can produce a handsome profit, we all must be especially conscientious about the origins of our work.

Cultural appropriation could be avoided in these ways:

1. Research the culture. Before you take something from a culture, it is wise to research how it originated and why it was

used by the marginalized group. Stereotypes are offensive and can cause much hurt, objectifying people and making them a monolith. Proper research shows how people are still individuals even though they are part of a larger group. Learn what is considered sacred by Black culture; those things should not be broached at all.[16]

2. Commit to investing in cultural competencies year-round. Support and celebrate Black life at more times than just Black History Month.[17]

3. Hire "Blackness consultants" to aid in the production of films and music that depict Black culture.[18] These individuals should be paid independently of the success of the work and should not be muzzled if and when the work comes out. These consultants should be involved in the content-creation process to ask the "why" when companies or groups want to take things from Black culture.[19] If it is simply for laughter or novelty in the larger white society, then consider what exactly the production is seeking to laugh at or make a novelty of. If it is to present something from Black life as the content creator's, with no regard to its origin, then, yes, that is theft of Black culture.

4. When criticized, listen instead of immediately going on the offensive. Marc Jacobs made a terrible mistake when he immediately responded to criticism for putting dreadlocks on white fashion models by criticizing Black women for straightening their hair. He later apologized, but a cool-down moment and a conversation with someone well versed in the hazards of cultural appropriation would have been wise.[20]

Action 21

Organize Annual Conversations on Deconstructing Race and Repairing the Harm

Because racism is the original sin of America and because virtually every problem we see now—from crime to poorly funded schools, environmental issues, poverty, technology gaps, wealth inequality, health disparities—can be traced back to some racial policy that was created to harm Black people, every organization should hold annual conversations and workshops on deconstructing race and repairing the harm it has done. Our society caused and created racism, then drafted policies to codify and social codes to enforce it. White supremacy did not create itself. Therefore, it will take a collective and repeated effort from all to deconstruct this sinful situation and find ways to repair the harm.

These conversations, which can take place at retreats or meals, can be a venue for drafting and adding language to the organization's bylaws and institutionalizing racial transformation (see action 23). In these conversations, people will have a chance to deeply discuss how we can jettison this belief in the hierarchy of human value based on the color of one's skin.

Some people may suggest that even having these conversations perpetuates racism, as if ignoring a four-hundred-year-old problem will simply make it go away. Other well-meaning people may take the conversation in a completely different direction so much so that nothing is done, decided, or deeply discussed as it relates to racism. There are other important justice issues; we do live in an intersectional world. But the issue of race and race alone deserves specific time to be unpacked and addressed. It seems America is far more willing to deliberate on every other topic but race and reparations. It's time for that day to end. Race and repair deserve their moment.

Action 22

Celebrate Juneteenth with an Annual Reparations Fundraiser

On June 16, 2021, Congress established Juneteenth as a national holiday. For the first time, the nation is celebrating what Blacks have since slavery ended. Juneteenth is America's true Independence Day—the commemoration of emancipation and the end of slavery. Notwithstanding that some Blacks got the news later and that some enslaved people of Native American tribes did not get freed until a year later, Juneteenth is celebrated June 19, the day enslaved people in Texas received their freedom.

This action calls for a celebration of Juneteenth in every city in America. Organizers will find ways to implement this observance, reaching out to churches, businesses, nonprofits, and other organizations in the community for sponsorship and activities. It is vitally important that the planning for this annual event should be led by a diverse board with African American leadership that can relate to the meaning of Juneteenth on a personal familial level.

Second, this proposal calls for annual Juneteenth reparations fundraising, through which people can donate money annually to a city reparations fund to benefit Blacks in the community, with the funds distributed according to whatever requirements the board sets. If the city later passes a reparations bill, then this board can choose whether to transfer funds to that account or to continue to run its distributions independently.

Juneteenth should teach us and remind us all that America had enslaved people and that though they were freed, they were never compensated or made whole from their work. Furthermore, it should remind everyone that the root cause of slavery—racism and white supremacy—continues to plague American society, multiplying the damage that continues without repair.

Action 23

Acknowledge Organizational Harm

In the four-hundred-plus-year period of pain and punishment for people of African descent in the United States of America, at no time has our pluralistic society spoken in unison to denounce its racist, sinful, and abominable actions. America has yet to repent for its original sin.

In every quarter of America, companies, organizations, nonprofits, and faith-based groups should have in their bylaws, policies, "about us" descriptions, or mission statements a section in which they acknowledge the gross harm American society has done to Black people. The statement can be placed near the Equal Employment Opportunity Commission (EEOC) statement prohibiting discrimination in the workplace, based on the 1964 Civil Rights Act. Just as the EEOC statement lets people know discrimination does not take place at this entity, employees, customers, visitors, and others should know *why* the organization does not discriminate.

It is not enough to say that the organization does not discriminate on the basis of race; it should also be stated that for more years than not, this young democracy made discrimination the law of the land. Be specific, because the oppression of Blacks and their suffering in this country stands alone in its own unique moral abyss. In the process of writing these statements, the group should interrogate its organizational history and impact for ways it has contributed to or benefited from racial injustice, and name what it pledges to do as a result.

Every segment of society must acknowledge the harm that Black people have gone through. This action serves to institutionalize the organization's solidarity with the plight of Blacks and their complete liberation and is even more important in the current age of revision of history. Today more than ever, this acknowledgment of harm needs to be presented, institutionalized, and made operational in every part of our society.

Action 24

Appoint Racial Equity Officers

This action calls for chamber of commerce offices across the country to have an office of racial equity, supervised by a racial equity officer who ensures that member businesses are practicing racial equity in hiring and assists in training them on the importance of the need for racial equity, understanding implicit bias and white fragility, and being a socially responsible corporate partner (or as I call it, a conscious corporate citizen). Moreover, each member of the chamber should have a racial equity officer to manage the growth and development of the work.

Racial equity is such an integral aspect of the work that needs to be done in corporate America. Blacks have been left out of upper management and denied employment, all the while helping to create the vast wealth of these major corporations. An important rubric to apply is that the corporation's leadership, employees, and board members should look like or come from the same community as their customers. Businesses in industries that have historically caused harm will be called on to make reparations; these offices of racial equity will be crucial for spearheading that work. Other industries will find that their expertise and connections will be ideally suited for contributing to the well-being and repair of the Black community.

Nonprofits should also have a racial equity officer to do similar work: overseeing the racial equity of their hiring, making sure employees are representative of those whom they serve, and finding learning opportunities for the nonprofit on all matters of racial equity. They should also aggregate data on all grant recipients and give reports to the board of directors.

Racial equity work should be institutionalized in the philanthropic and corporate segments of our society to make sure all organizations are aware of racial issues and have a staff that mirrors those they serve. Having such systems in place will encourage corporations and nonprofits to see their clients and patrons as people not merely to be sold to or assisted but to be hired and seen as colleagues. For those who claim they cannot find the funds to implement this action, consider that most corporations spend more on public relations than they do on racial equity. What matters more: how the company is perceived or what it actually does? For most, I think the problem is not the money but the will.

Action 25

Make Corporate Donations to Reparations

Private businesses have always supported causes they feel match their vision and mission. Corporate philanthropy has been a major buttress of good causes. Matching donations have helped increase and incentivize the gifts of individual donors. Corporations have created nonprofits and been premium sponsors of nonprofits for decades.

This action calls for corporations to make meaningful donations toward the cause of reparations. Companies that in the past benefited from slavery or have been found guilty of racist practices should be the first to make donations to such a fund.

A plethora of corporations, like Ben and Jerry's, already donate to social justice and reparatory justice causes. Corporate-backed nonprofits can also do great work in and around the cause of repair; for example, the Kellogg Foundation gives money to fight racism in its Truth, Racial Healing, and Transformation program. We need more organizations that are willing to make sound investments in the Black community as we as a society of people of goodwill seek to repair the harms of racism. I can think of no nobler a mission nor a more effective goal in community development or revitalization than to assist Black people in overcoming the perplexing obstacles of racism and the manifestations thereof both historically and in the present day.

Strategies for corporations' reparations campaigns would be similar to those for other causes they support: Donations can be made by the corporations, their employees, or their patrons. Patrons can pay extra for certain cause-specific products and services. For example, restaurants can have a five-cents reparations fee on certain drinks or meals. Retailers can add to the checkout line a donation option. Shoe and clothing companies can create a line of social justice apparel using slogans, such as "Reparations Now," with a portion of the proceeds going toward the reparations fund.

Action 26

Sponsor African American Family Reunions

Family reunions are commonplace in the Black community. Every summer, families travel from miles away to reconnect with each other. Reunions have become a staple in Black culture, helping to create family trees, compare genealogical research, extend fellowship, provide benevolent aid to family members in need, and educate youth on family heritage. Enjoying fellowship; playing games such as spades, dominoes, basketball, or football; and eating good food are hallmarks of a great family reunion.

Historically, family reunions have been taking place ever since emancipation. Virtually the first thing the newly freed enslaved people did was seek to reconnect with their families. Slavery was barbaric and debilitating for Black families. Children were ripped out of their crying mothers' hands and sold to plantation owners hundreds of miles away. Husbands were sold away from their wives. Marriages between enslaved people were not recognized legally, and minors had no protections against sexual violence. Black enslaved children were molested without any recourse. Reparations for these past crimes include supporting Black families.

Often when one enslaved person gained independence, they rapidly sought to purchase the freedom of their family. What was the point in being free if you could not be with your family? It is easy to see why, immediately after emancipation, formerly enslaved persons searched and found each other in what has become known as the family reunion. Ever since then Black families have set aside time to reunite the family. These reunions mean even more after the months and even years families were kept apart during the COVID-19 pandemic.

This proposal calls for these family reunions to be sponsored by those in the society who value repairing the family structure that was torn and deeply fractured during slavery. Travel companies, descendants of slave owners, hotels, caterers, airlines, or any groups of people who are sympathetic to this cause can sponsor or subsidize these family reunions.

Action 27

Sponsor African American Trips to Africa

Visiting your ancestral home has a profound impact on your life. I will never forget the time I visited the continent of Africa, affectionately known as the motherland. Its fills one with self-confidence, optimism, and a sense of rootedness. Where you are from is a significant part of who you are.

When Blacks were kidnapped from Africa and enslaved, they lost all connection with their homeland. Sponsoring the trip of an African American to visit Africa can go a long way to repair that rift and loss that many descendants of enslaved people still feel. If the trip can be planned in conjunction with genealogical study and if the beneficiary can identify the precise region of the continent from which they are primarily descended, the psychological benefit is enhanced even further. Travel agencies, airlines, and other businesses in the hospitality industry are ideally suited to provide this form of reparations.

Supporting an African American's visit to Africa has numerous benefits: in addition to the educational enrichment that helps to fill the void of forced separation for descendants of enslaved people, there is the mental health benefit of a free vacation for African Americans who often suffer minority stress, and the benefit of supporting African countries economically with tourism dollars.

Action 28

Demand Reparations from Medical Research Companies

Blacks have been the guinea pigs of American medicine since being kidnapped from our mother continent. Many modern medical insights and treatments owe their origins to the exploitation of African Americans. Such experimentation began during the time of slavery when researchers needed only the permission of owners to perform excruciating experimental procedures on enslaved people. J. Marion Sims, considered the father of modern gynecology, experimented on countless Black enslaved women in my home state of Alabama. By slicing and sewing women without anesthesia and without regard for their pain, dignity, or future health, he developed a surgical procedure to prevent a common childbirth complication and is lauded for his contributions. Only recently has the vile inhumanity of his research come under scrutiny.[21]

More recently, cancer cells taken without consent from Henrietta Lacks in 1951 were used to create a polio vaccine and to test cancer treatments at Johns Hopkins University Hospital in Baltimore, Maryland, where I now live. After Mrs. Lacks went to the hospital for help concerning vaginal bleeding, the doctors took tissue from her body without her knowledge or consent. Recognizing how resilient the cells were, researchers used them without her consent to study several diseases and formulate various drugs. Henrietta Lacks's cells, "commonly known as 'HeLa' cells, have been instrumental in the advancement of modern medicine and were used to develop the polio vaccine and in vitro fertilization, among myriad other innovations."[22] One company, Thermo Fisher Scientific, was sued by her estate for the massive profits it made off HeLa cells. In 2020, the company's revenue was $32.22 billion.[23]

My own hometown, Tuskegee, Alabama, is the site of the most infamous abuses in medical research. The "Tuskegee Study of Untreated Syphilis in the Negro Male," conducted for forty years, involved uninformed consent, deception, and outright racism. From 1932 to 1972, the US government studied 399 Black men with syphilis under the guise of providing them with free medical treatment because they had "bad blood." Even after penicillin became standard treatment for syphilis in 1947, the medicine was withheld from Tuskegee subjects because the researchers were studying *untreated* Syphilis. The experiment was stopped only because it was made public by Jean Heller of the Associated Press in 1972.[24]

This past injustice can and should be corrected by proper medical attention that does not exploit but cares for African Americans. Subsidized health care will require government action (see action step 74), but private pharmaceutical companies, a $1.48 *trillion* industry,[25] have a responsibility to repay the descendants of those on whom their profits were originally built. Pharmaceutical companies must identify the descendants of African Americans who were historically exploited for the sake of medicines from which they now profit and offer reparations by making prescription drugs free to those descendants. Consumers en masse must compel the health-care industry, in partnership with public agencies and philanthropic organizations, to help decrease the health disparities in Black communities by sponsoring people's health insurance premiums, co-pays, prescription drug costs, and medical bills.

Action 29

Demand Reparations from Energy Companies

The top three forms of energy utilized in the United States are fossil fuels (natural gas, petroleum, coal), nuclear energy, and renewable energy (biomass, hydropower, wind, solar, geothermal).

The energy industry, especially oil, has a racist history, including land theft, discriminatory hiring practices, and environmental racism. Energy is found on land that America systematically has stolen from Native Americans and Blacks whenever they felt it was valuable or needed for other purposes.[26] This action calls on energy companies to repair the harm by, first, fully compensating people for the property that was taken from them, people such as the descendants of William Godfrey in Chambers County, Texas, who was cheated and forced off his land by white men with guns. Today just one of those fields of his has produced 177 million barrels of oil.[27]

In 1996, Texaco entered into a $176 million settlement of a class action for racial discrimination against its employees.[28] In 2022 the five major oil companies, ExxonMobil, Shell, Chevron, BP, and TotalEnergies, made an average annual profit of $45 billion.[29] This is inexcusable, especially when you consider how much the oil and gas industry relies on tax breaks and exemptions to locate in various places, using as a rationale they would bring jobs and hire individuals from the local community—but not Black people, apparently.

The historical racist hiring practices that either left Blacks out or hired them only for hazardous, hard labor have set the current environment. The coal mining industry has placed debilitating burdens on the backs of Blacks who dug the mines and went deep into the earth, but once modern technology came and better tools were invented, many Blacks were discharged while the whites stayed with the companies.

In the field of nuclear energy, uranium enrichment facilities at Oak Ridge, Tennessee, and in other cities that were part of the Manhattan Project during World War II practiced racial discrimination. Living segregated from the whites in meager "hutments," even separated from their spouses, Black workers were "generally only allowed to occupy the lowest paying jobs."[30] Also in the nuclear field, a study in the 1960s and early 1970s was designed to evaluate the radiation exposure soldiers could safely receive. Eighty-two charity cancer patients at the University of Cincinnati Medical Center, three-quarters of whom were Black men and women, were exposed to severe full-body and partial radiation. Within the first sixty days after exposure, twenty-five of the patients died.[31]

In addition, the energy industry is responsible for much of the pollution that primarily affects Black communities (see action 77). The oil and gas industry produces eight million metric tons of methane annually, as well as volatile organic compounds and hydrogen sulfide gas.[32]

Due to the abuse inflicted on Blacks by the energy field, action 29 calls for every Black household in America to receive $100 off their monthly utility bill and a gas card worth $5,200 ($100 a week) to be used for gasoline. Funds also need to be made available so that Black homes can be made more energy efficient. Oversight for this program should ensure that reparative actions are not shortsighted, understanding the impact of racism on homeownership, which is required for certain energy solutions. For example, California has a program to subsidize a home charging station for people who purchase an electric car.[33] However, only 36.2 percent of Black residents of California own their homes, so many do not qualify for the rebate.[34] The initiative for solar rooftop systems is similar: studies show it overwhelmingly has benefited white households much more than Blacks.[35]

"Clean energy and solar need to be cognizant of the fact that we're operating in an energy system that is intertwined with lots of other systems that are racist at their core," said Melanie Santiago-Mosier, managing director for access and equity for Vote Solar, an organization that advocates for solar energy. "We need to be very careful that as we grow and mature, we're not replicating the injustices that have proliferated to date throughout the energy system."[36]

Action 30

Toughen Social Media Restrictions on Hate Speech

In the last twenty years, social media has become the primary channel for communication, surpassing phone calls and even email. Social media is where people connect and reconnect with friends and family, watch videos, scroll through pictures; where churches broadcast services; where information and news are shared.

Because people spend an exorbitant amount of time on social

media, it has also replaced news stations and newspapers as the source people go to for information on what is happening in the world. Such a change would not be so harmful if there were any sort of vetting process before comments were posted. However, there is not. As a result, social media has been the depository of salacious, seditious shards of truth at best and sinfully shameful lies at worst. Social media has its share of sardonic satire, which occasionally spreads like the gospel, and often the theories espoused on social media make it onto the mainstream platforms. Sometimes it seems as though mainstream media is more influenced by social media than social media is influenced by it.

Individuals, including minors, terrorists, and foreign governments, can create fake accounts and post all sorts of false and misleading content. Consider how common it became for people to believe the lie that President Obama was not born in the United States or that the 2020 election was "rigged." Similarly, anyone can claim to be spouting scientific fact and say that Blacks are less human than whites or that whites are being replaced by other ethnicities, and those insidious posts can stay up unless someone reports them—and even then, nothing might be done. These lies have led to real-life acts of terrorism by racist white supremacists. Social media has become a cesspool of unverified, unsupported statements made by unverified people. The dearth of Blacks working in Silicon Valley in executive positions is part of the problem, as those in charge do not feel the impact of racist hate speech.

To stop the damage and repair this harm, social media companies should (1) employ more Blacks in executive positions, (2) establish free coding camps in urban and rural cities, particularly for Black youth, (3) offer training sites for adults looking for jobs in computer technology, (4) make it easier for web creators to monetize their ingenuity to ensure that profits for their posts go to the creators, not the social media companies, (5) search for and delete racist hate speech and deactivate accounts and ban email addresses and IP numbers for those who post or spread racist hate speech, and (6) verify accounts, making sure all accounts are from real people.

Action 31

Offer Free After-School Tutoring and Enrichment

The education of children is paramount to their development. In recent decades it has been made abundantly clear that all school-age children need more support than is currently available at most public schools. Black youth are more likely to be in public schools that have overcrowded classrooms and lack funding for special programs.

Booker T. Washington said in 1915 that "white men will vote funds for Negro education just in proportion to their belief in the value of that education."[37] Sadly, that statement still holds true, as Black children attend poorly funded schools, and their parents most likely did as well. In poorly funded schools, classes are over-crowded, teachers are less qualified, and program offerings are at a bare minimum. Therefore, the basic level of education is simply not always there.

This is a legacy of educational racism. During slavery it was against the law for enslaved people to even know how to read and write. After slavery, Blacks attended Jim Crow schools that taught them only the skills needed to wash clothes and be sharecroppers. This model was never meant to help provide equality but to keep Black youth subservient to whites.

This action calls on nonprofits like educational foundations, church groups, and the public school system itself to offer free after-school tutorial programs to Black children in repair of the gross damage done educationally to them, their parents, their grand-parents, and their ancestors. In these after-school programs, students will be tutored in their subjects, given advanced work, and taught life skills, entrepreneurship, and sound financial strategies. Organizations unable to support the effort financially can send people to do the actual tutoring and teach the lessons. In the summer, the program can offer continued educational enrichment as well as sports and other physical activities.

Action 32

Teach Black History and Culture

Black history is one of the least-known topics in the country. Being in Tulsa and seeing with my own eyes how few people knew about the 1921 Tulsa Race Massacre was astonishing. Lawyers, doctors, national figures were flabbergasted that they were never taught about it. Even history majors and civil rights activists were stunned that they were never taught about the 1921 violence.

Ignorance of the Tulsa massacre is apropos to the overall approach to the history of Black people. Remarkably little African American history is included in American history curricula, and virtually no African history is shared in world history courses. Meanwhile, European history dominates world history courses, and American social studies curriculum obfuscates the sins of European Americans. In the textbooks of some states, such as Texas, enslaved people are referred to as "migrant workers." Enslaved Blacks were not migrant workers. Workers have a choice as to whether they accept a job; the enslaved did not have the luxury of turning down a job that they were never paid to do. Such a gross mischaracterization is not unusual here in America as it glosses over a past that it would like to forget.

Even more unfortunate than misrepresenting enslavement is the implication that Black history began with slavery. Reducing the history of Black people to about three hundred years, most history books make no mention of Black history or culture prior to America. Black achievement and African history are not taught at all.

Not knowing Black history in all its fullness deprives America and Black people of knowing more about their heritage. As a result, Black people have a lower sense of self-worth. When people do not know themselves fully, they cannot expect to be fully known, and when that happens, it is easier to hurt, harm, or kill them because they are seen as of less value. The restraint police officers show with armed whites who have killed innocent Black people is staggering. Dylann Roof, who had just shot and killed people at Mother Emanuel AME Church in Charleston, South Carolina, was not only apprehended alive but was taken to Burger King to get something to eat. Payton Gendron, who killed ten Black people at Tops grocery store in Buffalo, New York, was armed when the police came on the scene, yet they arrested him without further incident. Compare this to police treatment of unarmed Black men like Eric Garner, George Floyd, and so many others, manifesting the disdain (or, at best, ambivalence) that many whites have toward Blacks.

Rather than revising school curricula to increase knowledge of and respect for Black heritage, many states are making it illegal to teach about race in America in a critical way. Instead of passing meaningful police reform that can save lives, state legislatures are passing laws to reduce talk about America's racial history—history Americans already know very little about.

This action calls on society to teach the full spectrum of Black history, not just slavery and a decontextualized chapter on the civil rights movement. Black history should be taught as an integral part of American and world history. From elementary through high school, schools should teach full and accurate history and should celebrate Black History Month and now Juneteenth with greater understanding of who we are as a people, what we've been through, and what we've achieved.

Chapter 3

Institutional Reparations

*I*nstitutional reparations involve the most comprehensive and truest form of justice and accountability. The racial injustice that has plagued our country since its very first days is not the responsibility of individuals acting alone or a few rogue groups. The injustice is systemic—interwoven in every aspect of American society—and therefore requires systemic solutions that can be enacted only by governmental institutions. Black Americans' loyalty has been shuttled between two political parties, neither of which has proffered a sustained, comprehensive plan of uplift, healing, and repair for Black people. Yet despite America's perfidious piety and perfunctory penchant for peace, Blacks have repeatedly laid panegyric at the feet of the United States of America all the while it had its feet on their necks.

Before 1865, the entire economy was based in large part on slave labor. Blacks picked cotton, tobacco, sugar cane, and other crops. Virtually every aspect of manual labor was done by Blacks for free in all the slave states, which also benefited northern factories and commerce. Free Blacks in the North were largely underpaid and constantly under threat of being shipped south due to the Fugitive Slave Law. The young, fragile, poor democracy of the United States of America financially needed slavery to produce in large scale the goods required to meet the world demand for cotton, tobacco, indigo, and other crops native to America. In total, more than 12.5 million Africans were taken and shipped to the Western Hemisphere to be sold as enslaved people, making it the largest mass transportation of any group of people in the history of the world.

Let's not forget who these valuable humans were before they were kidnapped and trafficked for the profit of other nations. They were kings, queens, noblemen, craftsmen, artisans, blacksmiths, fishermen, scribes, medicine men, scholars, philosophers, religious leaders, and more. They were members of communities with a rich culture and seemingly unlimited resources. They attended school, danced, and laughed. Africans were happy where they were and did not feel the need to seek relocation. Their land was more than sufficient. Oftentimes, in reparations discussions, we calculate and quantify the labor of the enslaved but seldom consider the life they had before arriving in America. So, in quantifying damages, we are leaving out a monumental asset in ignoring the value of the life that was snatched from them, their life and the land they dwelled on before slavery. Europeans did not kidnap enslaved people, they kidnapped millionaires and made them peasants. They bought free men and women, boys and girls, and made them into enslaved people. People are bought—enslaved people are made.

This chapter aims to summarize some of the heinous ways African Americans were robbed of their freedom, health, and labor, and how—even after emancipation—we have been systemically hindered in our efforts to restore our people to the thriving life our ancestors once had.

Stolen Life and Liberty

Torture began at the moment of capture. Chains put on the newly captured humans were their first introduction to life as an enslaved person. In the dungeon or point of no return, chains attached them to walls. Chains were on them as they slept, ate, used the bathroom on themselves, and of course when they were chained together in the belly of a ship, right next to and on top of each other. Slave ships were built for carrying as much cargo as possible, not providing comfort, so there was little to no ventilation and no place to use the restroom, creating a hot, stinking cesspool of disease. It was said the ships could be smelled several miles away. Death was a common occurrence, and the bodies of the dead were discarded overboard. Jumping overboard when brought above deck for exercise was so common that sharks followed the slave ships to feast on those who jumped to their deaths or those who died from disease or murder. It has been observed by zoologists that the route of the Middle Passage from Africa to the New World changed the migration pattern of sharks in the Atlantic Ocean.

When the recently captured Africans finally made it to America, they were forced to walk from the ship dock to the auction block, naked and in chains, a miles-long trek in some cases. Once on the auction block, these Africans were poked and prodded, examined in the mouth and private parts, their strength was tested—whatever a potential buyer wanted to do. There were no laws governing this stolen cargo—no United Nations human rights violations to consider, no Civil Rights Division of the Justice Department, no immigration office. These enslaved persons were completely helpless, sold away from spouses and children, given new names, and forbidden to retain their own language, religion, and culture.

The Middle Passage, auction block, and violent erasure of humanity is what made American slavery unique. Never before in the history of the world were people kidnapped and shipped overseas so far from their home. In many other contexts from the time of antiquity, enslaved people could still practice their religion (consider the biblical stories of Joseph, Daniel, and the three Hebrews), familial bonds were left intact, and enslaved people could often earn money working other jobs. In America, enslaved people had no rights, no property, no free time, save perhaps a few hours on Sunday when they could worship with their "master" or hear from an approved preacher. Living conditions were wretched, beatings were given to intimidate and send messages to the others enslaved on the plantation, and captured runaways could be castrated or have their foot cut off. Enslaved people, including children, were raped routinely and could be sold at any time without concern for family bonds. Sickness was rampant; infant mortality was high. The enslaved always lived under the threat of violence and were forbidden from knowing how to read or write.

Oppressed though Free

Abraham Lincoln's Emancipation Proclamation took effect on January 1, 1863, and while many enslaved African Americans remained in captivity until closer to the end of the Civil War, the promise of freedom marked a turning point.

Following his scorched-earth campaign through Atlanta to the sea in late 1864, General William T. Sherman received approval from Secretary of War Edwin Stanton to meet with leaders of the Black community. About twenty leaders, mostly pastors, met with Sherman in Savannah, Georgia. General Sherman asked what they wanted as newly freed Americans, and the men said to just give them land and they would take care of themselves. Sherman had just seized about four hundred thousand acres from plantation owners along the coast from South Carolina to Florida. They had enough land to give the newly freed enslaved people forty acres per family and, later, a mule. Senators such as Thaddeus Stevens and Charles Sumner supported the plan and pushed President Lincoln to establish the Bureau of Refugees, Freedmen, and Abandoned Lands, later known as the Freedmen's Bureau, in March 1865. Little over a month later, however, on April 14, 1865, President Lincoln was assassinated and Andrew Johnson, a southern apologist, became president. Johnson pardoned Confederates, returned land to the plantation owners, and allowed southern states to enact harsh "black codes" restricting the behavior and limiting the prospects of the formerly enslaved.

Northern voters and legislators were outraged by the black codes and managed to implement some of the goals of Reconstruction in spite of Johnson.[1] More than fifteen hundred freedmen held elected office between 1865 and 1877, during which time the first public schools in the South were established and laws against racial discrimination were passed. This era of progress was short-lived, however, because of violent backlash to these revolutionary changes and the presidency of former Union general Ulysses S. Grant. Republican support for Reconstruction waned, and southern Democrats gained control of both Congress and most state legislatures in the South. With the compromise of 1876, Reconstruction officially ended, and Black people never have been close to any sort of repair ever since. The US government has failed us.

All the protection the freed enslaved people had was evaporated and the black codes were expanded to ensure that Blacks could not rise to any semblance of prominence again. These laws restricted Blacks' way of life. Ultimately, they criminalized Black behavior, while the Thirteenth Amendment making slavery illegal kept a provision for slavery "as a punishment for crime." They made it illegal to not have a job, knowing that Blacks owned no companies and that whites had to hire them, and only former plantation owners would. With the nascent Ku Klux Klan as well as the first police forces to strike terror in the hearts of Blacks, freedmen were assaulted, disenfranchised, criminalized, terrorized, and sometimes even re-enslaved.

Seeking a Place to Thrive

During this same era, in which the US government failed to fulfill its promise of even just forty acres to Black families, it was simultaneously giving away millions of acres in both the South and across the Great Plains through the Homestead Acts, beginning in 1862 and expanded in 1866 and 1909.[2] By the time the acts expired in 1934, more than 1.5 million white families had received 160-acre plots of land, while a generous estimate indicates fewer than nine thousand Black families benefited.[3]

Even without government assistance, many Blacks left the Klan-controlled South in the decades surrounding the turn of the twentieth century, traveling north, east, and west to finally taste a piece of the American pie. Especially after 1910, during a period known as the Great Migration, these political refugees migrated everywhere but farther south, and in their new cities formed churches, schools, mutual aid societies, service businesses such as funeral homes and beauty parlors, transportation services, and some professional offices such as lawyers and doctors. Jim Crow laws barring Blacks from white-owned businesses meant that they had at least their demographic to count on to support their enterprises, which became so lucrative that everywhere these Blacks went they created their own Black Wall Street (or Little Africa, as it was called by whites). Even outside the South, however, some whites were threatened by seeing Blacks as successful business professionals. Well-off whites who were underpaying poor whites, especially recent immigrants from Europe, manipulated the pain and poverty of the white Europeans to place blame on the newly arriving Blacks for their problems. Racism fueled economic jealousy, and the country was a powder keg.

The First World War increased demand for workers and services, as well as young men to fight. When the war ended in 1919, there was a thriving Black middle class, and Black soldiers who had risked their lives for the United States were coming home and being treated as second-class citizens. But these men had newfound dignity after wearing the uniforms of their country and receiving some modicum of respect overseas. As discussed in the introduction, the dissonance of Black men seen as "boys" in the eyes of whites more boldly exerting themselves as men made the steady flow of Jim Crow racial violence explode into a flood of race massacres. They occurred all over America: Tulsa, East St. Louis, New Orleans, Philadelphia, Chicago, Rosewood, New York City, Atlanta, Knoxville, Elaine, Washington, DC, and Harlem, to name a few. The summer of 1919 was called Red Summer because of the bloodshed. Despite the immense loss of Black life and property, no white people were ever convicted and punished for their violent actions. Instead, police arrested Blacks in the aftermath and referred to the massacres as riots.

When the era of the most overt racial terror (1900–35) subsided, institutions codified ways to inhibit Black progress. Whites managed to segregate Blacks into certain areas of town without a legal mandate through the practice of redlining. Banks drew maps of the city, color-coding neighborhoods based on the risk level of the investments. Colors indicated not only the wealth of current residents but their religion and race. Areas shaded green were populated by white homeowners, mostly Protestant Christians (depending on the status of Catholics and Jews in each city); blue and yellow indicated some level of caution; areas shaded red, populated by Blacks, were labeled a "hazardous" investment. When the government implemented the New Deal to deliver America out of the grips of the Depression, one benefit was government-backed home loans, but because the government-sponsored Home Owners' Loan

Corporation and because the Federal Home Loan Bank Board used those color-coded maps, many Black Americans were denied loans, even if their income indicated they could easily make their mortgage payments.[4] Redlining had such a devastating effect that the red-shaded neighborhoods on maps drawn in the 1930s are still where the overwhelming number of Black people live today, without the generational wealth that comes from homeownership.

The New Deal was a major transformative moment in American politics and included staple programs such as Social Security and the federal minimum wage. Although at the time Blacks were typically Republican because it was the party of Abraham Lincoln, in 1936, 75 percent of Black voters chose to support Democrats in large part because they felt the Republicans were starting to take their votes for granted and because President Franklin Roosevelt spoke to more ways of helping the poor and bringing the nation out of the Great Depression. Regretfully, Roosevelt's New Deal revealed America's old problem with racism, and Blacks lost out on many of its benefits.[5] Actions 34–37 will explain the impact of this exclusion in more detail.

In another historic social program of the US government, the GI Bill was passed in 1944 to assist soldiers returning from World War II with buying homes, starting businesses, and paying for higher education. Its benefits are largely responsible for the economic boom of the 1950s, including the growth of the suburbs and the high rate of homeownership. Troublingly, but not surprisingly, Black veterans did not benefit as much from it as white veterans and their families, and many did not benefit at all.

As was the case with the New Deal a decade earlier, racist southern Democrats ensured that language was put into the bill to prevent across-the-board implementation that would elevate the status of many African American veterans. Lawmakers like Mississippi Congressman John Rankin inserted into the bill that GI Bill funds should be administered by the states and not the federal government. He knew that states like Mississippi would not give Blacks equal access to the funds. Some postmasters would not send GI Bill–related mail to the houses of Black veterans. Many colleges and universities did not admit Black students at the time, and the Historically Black Colleges and Universities (HBCUs) were already underfunded and could not handle a large influx of students, never mind the fact that many Black veterans did not utilize the educational benefits because a college degree seemed to be a luxury to men who needed a job urgently.

While 4.3 million low-interest home loans were given in the decade following the passing of the GI Bill, elevating or cementing millions of white families into the middle class, Black families were left behind.[6] As political scientist Ira Katznelson stated, there was "no greater instrument for widening an already huge racial gap in postwar America than the GI Bill."[7]

Community Destabilization

In addition to the financial exploitation present throughout African Americans' history, the US government's acts of racial terror have hindered Blacks emotionally and politically. America's hateful war on Black people has hurt our ability to build capacity and strong community. Blacks have lost not only homes, money, and land but also leaders. Throughout our fight for freedom and prosperity, figures have risen to lead the charge, and white America has attacked those who sought to bring solutions and advocate for peace and healing. One of the worst psychological blows inflicted on the Black community since racial terror at the beginning of the nineteenth century is the assassinations both physically and politically of any leader who dared speak to racial equality or liberation for Blacks. Malcolm X, Medgar Evers, the Rev. Dr. Martin Luther King Jr., Fred Hampton, and so many other civil rights activists and freedom fighters were killed. This left a void in the leadership structure that has not since been filled. Sadly, many believe the mastermind behind these killings was J. Edgar Hoover's Federal Bureau of Investigation (FBI)—that it planned, or at least knew about and could have thwarted, attempts on the lives of these leaders.

The Black Panthers were undermined and taken down by the government through COINTELPRO, an FBI counterintelligence program run from 1956 to 1971 "to discredit and neutralize organizations considered subversive to US political stability."[8] Because most of the files remain sealed and because much of what has been released is heavily redacted, the American people still do not know all that was done by the US government to Black people, but a 1975 Senate select committee formed to investigate intelligence activities reported,

> Many of the techniques used would be intolerable in a demo-cratic society even if all of the targets had been involved in violent activity, but COINTELPRO went far beyond that. . . . The Bureau conducted a sophisticated vigilante operation aimed squarely at preventing the exercise of First Amendment rights of speech and association, on the theory that preventing the growth of dangerous groups and the propagation of dangerous ideas would protect the national security and deter violence.[9]

With many of our leaders assassinated, intimidated into silence, or wrongly imprisoned, it is no wonder that it seems our communities are in a tailspin. But that perception is more myth than fact. And the facts presented have inconvenient truths behind them that are rarely reported. The news shows the rate of violent crime, but it does not explore how those guns got into our communities in the first place. The news shows the big drug bust in communities of color, but it doesn't mention how, according to reports, cocaine was allowed to enter the United States.

It is indisputable that the CIA worked closely with Contra leaders who were trafficking drugs in order to buy weapons during the 1980s conflict in Nicaragua. Frederick P. Hitz, the CIA inspector general, testified before the House Intelligence Committee in 1998 that the US agency was at the very least a bystander to the smuggling of cocaine. The question of how involved the CIA was and with what intent has been a matter of immense speculation for decades, with some investigators linking the Contra traffickers directly to Los Angeles drug boss "Freeway" Ricky Ross and the explosion of crack cocaine in the city. Most media outlets shied away from directly implicating the CIA, however, and retrospectives on the debate concluded that "journalism more or less ate itself while the government mostly skipped away with its secret doings intact."[10]

At the same time the government turned a blind eye to the trafficking of cocaine, Ronald Reagan declared a "war on drugs," saying narcotics were a "threat to U.S. national security."[11] This was in 1982, when drug use and drug crime were actually on the decline, but the campaign was a political strategy to appeal to whites in the South upset with the gains of Blacks following integration.

It's clear to me that the drugs were brought here and placed in our communities in an act of chemical warfare that Blacks are still devastated by. As Michelle Alexander asserts in her best-selling book *The New Jim Crow: Mass Incarceration in the Age of Colorblindness*, prisons are disproportionately filled with Black people because this so-called war on drugs unfairly criminalizes Black people.[12] Black communities are policed more stringently than whites' (even though the rate of drug use is similar in Black and white populations) and laws penalize drugs popular among Black users (such as crack cocaine) much more severely than those popular with white users (powdered cocaine)—one hundred times more severely, according to Alexander. "A conviction for the sale of five hundred grams of powder cocaine triggers a five-year mandatory sentence, while only five grams of crack triggers the same sentence."[13] There are more Black adults under "correctional control" (in prison, in jail, or on parole) today than were enslaved in 1850. Due to the incarceration of so many in our community, more Black people were disenfranchised in 2004 than in 1870, and Black children are less likely to be raised by two parents today than during slavery.[14]

Institutional Reparations Are Owed

While many white conservatives insist that they achieved their success or stability on their own, it is clear that government programs subsidized the quality of life their parents or grandparents attained, which had generational impact. Financial support from government institutions is not a new or "communist" concept, as some would suggest. While the wealth of rulers and royals in predemocratic times was often hoarded at the top, the Bible tells of a major support package that King Cyrus of Persia gave to the Jews freed from the Babylonian exile.

When Cyrus the Great defeated the Babylonians, he told the leaders of the Jewish community,

> Any of you who are [God's] people may go to Jerusalem in Judah to rebuild this Temple of the LORD, the God of Israel, who lives in Jerusalem. And may your God be with you! Wherever this Jewish remnant is found, let their neighbors contribute toward their expenses by giving them silver and gold, supplies for the journey, and livestock, as well as a voluntary offering for the Temple of God in Jerusalem. (Ezra 1:3–4 NLT)

The Persians gave repair even though they were not the ones who took the Israelites out of Jerusalem; the people of Persia paid taxes and made gifts supporting this effort. Cyrus even located the items the Babylonians had taken from the Jewish temple in their siege and returned them. "In all, there were 5,400 articles of gold and silver," says verse 11 (NLT). That is repair.

A century later, when the prophet Nehemiah was planning his return to Jerusalem, he asked the Persian king, Artaxerxes,

> "If it please the king, let me have letters addressed to the governors of the province west of the Euphrates River, instructing them to let me travel safely through their territories on my way to Judah. And please give me a letter addressed to Asaph, the manager of the king's forest, instructing him to give me timber. I will need it to make beams for the gates of the Temple fortress, for the city walls, and for a house for myself." And the king granted these requests, because the gracious hand of God was on me.
>
> When I came to the governors of the province west of the Euphrates River, I delivered the king's letters to them. The king, I should add, had sent along army officers and horsemen to protect me. (Neh. 2:7–9 NLT)

Artaxerxes did not destroy the temple nor take the Israelites away, but he was charged with addressing the issue because he was in possession of a stolen people. Not only did he supply them resources, King Artaxerxes provided protection so that the Israelites could exercise their freedom in peace.

Do not African Americans, who were brought to this land as a stolen people, deserve the full and generous support of their government? Despite the horrors and heartbreaks inflicted on them, Blacks have remained steadfast in their love and fidelity toward America. Like a person loving an abusive spouse, Blacks have loved America until America has taken their resources, impacted their mental health, taken advantage of their children, and, yes, ultimately killed them. Proving their unquestioned patriotism in every war that America has fought, Blacks have fought valiantly. Incidentally, the very first person who lost his life for America was a Black man named Crispus Attucks during the American Revolution.

On top of their military service, since emancipation Blacks have paid taxes to America, on federal, state, and local levels. The tax dollars they paid have gone to police departments that assaulted them, to fire departments that turned a blind eye during massacres, to operation of elections they could not vote in, and to construction of highways that demolished their communities. Their tax dollars have gone to build schools that their children could not attend, libraries they could not enter, and pools they could not swim in. Blacks have paid taxes to the American government since emancipation and have yet to truly receive benefit of their tax dollars nor a refund. In fact, in most states, because a regressive tax system levies sales tax on necessities while keeping income taxes low or nonexistent to benefit the wealthy, Blacks pay a higher proportion of their income in tax than other groups.

Because of these grievances, historical injustices, and societal failings, reparations do not address only the effects of slavery but also all the harm to Blacks in the 160-plus years since emancipation. What follows are descriptions of what the United States can proffer in terms of relief.

Action 33

Establish a Reparatory Justice Oversight Committee

Institutional reparations require the work of government agencies. A reparatory justice oversight committee is a necessary first step for coordinating and providing accountability for the implementation of a national plan of reparations.

President Joe Biden's Executive Order 13985, officially titled Advancing Racial Equity and Support for Underserved Communities through the Federal Government, was the first order of his presidency. It calls for "an ambitious whole-of-government equity agenda that matches the scale of the opportunities and challenges that we face."[15] Under this executive order, each agency has to deliver on measurable objectives as it relates to building equity for marginalized groups in America.

Action 33 builds on this executive order by creating a specific department of reparatory oversight that monitors each agency's progress not just in providing equitable relief to Blacks but also in repairing the harm caused by centuries of racism and discrimination.

The Department of the Treasury in particular will play a monumental role in providing repair to Blacks. For everything listed in this book that has a governmental monetary cost, it will be the role of the secretary of the treasury to ensure that the financial plan of reparations is administered and distributed adequately. A model for such a committee is the Treasury Advisory Committee on Racial Equity formed by the current secretary, Janet Yellen. Its goal is to "provide advice and recommendations to Secretary Yellen and Deputy Secretary Wally Adeyemo on efforts to advance racial equity in the economy and address acute disparities for communities of color."[16]

This action calls on a similar committee to be formed to provide advice and oversight to all appropriate departments on ways to repair the financial harm done to Black people in this country, including loss of wages due to slavery and black codes, loss of wealth due to higher interest rates and lower home value from redlining, poorly funded schools, discrimination that prevented Blacks from getting an education or entry into a financially lucrative career, racial terror against Black businesses, unpaid insurance claims, and so much more.

Action 34

Finance Black Homeownership

Knowing that homeownership is foundational to building wealth, the New Deal's architects sought to accelerate homeownership and encourage banks to lend to aspiring home buyers. So, the federal government, through the newly formed Federal Housing Authority (FHA), would guarantee mortgages by backing the loan. Blacks were excluded from participating in and receiving FHA loans through discriminatory practices like redlining and contract leasing. "Only two percent of the $120 billion in new housing subsidized by the federal government between 1934 and 1962 went to nonwhites."[17]

Houses in predominantly Black neighborhoods are appraised at a lower value simply because Blacks live there, and yet they are over-assessed for tax purposes.[18] This raises expenses for individual families while tax revenue compared to wealthier areas remains low, which means fewer public services and less funding for schools, which leads to poorer education, which means less access to better-paying jobs, leading to high unemployment and high poverty, which leads to high crime, and high crime leads back to lower property value—a cycle that has continued for decades. It all started with the federal government and its racist policies.

This all has had a major effect on increasing the wealth gap between Blacks and whites. Several banks have been sued and had to pay large settlements because they discriminated against Blacks by charging them a higher interest rate or refused to give them a mortgage. "The average Black homeowner's interest rate is 33 basis points higher than the average white homeowner, and Black homeowners pay about $250 more per year in interest charges."[19] For all these reasons, it should be no surprise that Blacks have the lowest homeownership rate of all ethnic groups at 45 percent.[20]

To repair the effects of governmental policies that have prevented

Black Americans from owning homes and therefore building the equity required for generational wealth, the United States must provide 100 percent government-backed loans with below-prime fixed interest rates, downpayment assistance, closing-cost assistance, and monthly mortgage payment emergency funds to assist Blacks in paying their mortgage when life crises happen. Blacks who are seeking to purchase a home should have to meet only the income requirements—not credit score nor debt-to-income ratio—in order to qualify for a mortgage.

Current homeowners should be allowed to refinance their mortgage at a rate at least 0.5 percent less than their current interest rate. This refinance should be done regardless of their credit score or debt-to-income ratio. In addition, the federal government should give Blacks 10 percent of the value of their home to use for improvements or debt elimination. Because of unfair lending practices, Blacks have not had the disposable income to make needed improvements to keep up the value of their houses or eliminate their debt.

Last, the Department of Housing and Urban Development (HUD) should make grants to Black builders and developers to create subsidized subdivisions in historically Black neighborhoods, helping to revitalize these communities without leading to displacement.[21]

Action 35

Make Restitution to Black Farmers

As explained in the introduction of chapter 3, land was to be given to the newly freed Blacks. Action 35 can help pay what America owed and promised to the freed Blacks after slavery and can also provide restitution for land that has been stolen from Blacks in the time since.

In May 1862, the federal government passed the Homestead Act, which ultimately gave away 270 million acres of land for a nominal fee, mostly to white Americans. In 1933, a New Deal policy paid landowning farmers subsidies *not* to produce in an effort to correct crop prices. "Since 40 percent of all black workers made their living as sharecroppers and tenant farmers, the Agricultural Adjustment Administration (AAA) acreage reduction hit Blacks hard. White landlords could make more money by leaving land untilled than by putting land back into production. As a result, the AAA's policies forced more than 100,000 blacks off the land in 1933 and 1934."[22]

Blacks who were able to obtain land and become farmers for themselves were often cheated and had land taken from them through government-sponsored farm programs that disenfranchised and discriminated against Black farmers. Most of this land theft occurred after 1950, sometimes as a backlash to the civil rights movement. Federal money was distributed to farmers through local US Department of Agriculture (USDA) boards, which were dominated by segregationists. Blacks were denied money if they were members of civil rights organizations, or voters, and so on.[23] "A war waged by deed of title has dispossessed 98 percent of black agricultural landowners in America," reports the *Atlantic*.[24]

Action 35 aims to return the land to Black families and to provide grants to Black farmers who were discriminated against by the USDA. These grants will go to purchase land and farm equipment. Partnership should be made with the Department of the Interior to make land of national parks available for Black farmers and descendants of Black farmers who were cheated out of land to farm. A department of reparatory justice should be established to oversee the work. Additionally, state agricultural departments will be responsible to make the same grants and establish an office of reparatory justice.

Action 36

Increase Minimum Wage and Employment Assistance

By the racist exclusion of African Americans from many New Deal programs, the majority of Blacks were left out of one of the best social safety nets in American history. This impact could be felt for generations to come.

For example, the National Industrial Recovery Act (NIRA) was designed to "spread available work among a larger number of workers by (a) limiting hours and launching a public works program and (b) increasing individuals' purchasing power by establishing minimum wage rates." It was administered in part by the National Recovery Administration (NRA).[25]

It ultimately gave preferential treatment to white job applicants and greatly reduced salary schedules and pay rates for Blacks. The system of regulated wage codes ignored the realities of Black workers; for example, it restricted the hours of hairdressers to the daytime, but most Black hairdressers worked in the evening, since their clientele often worked domestic jobs during the day. Regulations on the cotton industry "excluded the central positions where black male workers labored, while the southern lumber industry's wages were far lower than those wages paid in the North. Even when black workers were eligible for higher wages, employers preferred to pay this money to white workers."[26]

To mitigate and address the disparities caused by the NRA, Black hourly wage employees should receive a $1 increase to their minimum wage for at least eighty-eight years (the time between the NIRA and when this action takes effect) along with job training and placement in urban and rural communities where Blacks are more than 50 percent of the population. Blacks who do not live there can travel to those sites to receive training for technology, construction, manufacturing, and other skilled jobs. Stipends will need to be given to the participants.

Action 37

Support Black Seniors

The third major New Deal policy that left out a majority of Blacks was Social Security. In fact, it left out half of the workforce in America by excluding agricultural and domestic workers. At the time, in 1935, 60 percent of African Americans worked in one of those two areas. While historians such as Linda Gordon feel this was intentional and in line with other New Deal programs that, in order to pass, had to be approved by southern Democrats who did not want to help Blacks in any way, other historians, such as

Larry DeWitt, say the exclusion of Blacks was only a happenstance because collecting Social Security tax from agricultural and domestic workers was harder to administrate.[27]

It is hard to imagine the Social Security Act's designers did not know these industries were largely made up of Black workers. These were the only nonthreatening jobs Blacks could obtain after slavery, having been limited by a society that made it against the law for them to read or write. Due to school segregation, discriminatory hiring practices, and intimidation by whites, namely the Ku Klux Klan, African Americans remained largely relegated to these industries well into the mid-twentieth century.

Because many African American seniors were denied jobs as younger adults that would have allowed them to pay into Social Security, many of them are now struggling or living in poverty. An individual could help repair this injustice by assisting an older African American with expenses, nursing home fees, home health, transportation, and grocery expenses. However, the impact of this deplorable government "oversight" is too large to repair through individual action.

To support Black seniors, this action calls on the US government through the Social Security Administration to provide $100,000 a year to pay for nursing home care, home health care, medical expenses, mortgage reduction, or groceries. As with the minimum wage increase, this action should last for at least eighty-eight years.

The Social Security Act was a monumental piece of legislation that opened the door for many white families who lived in poverty during the Great Depression to financially recover, building a foundation for wealth and prosperity for years to come. Repairing this failure requires attention to the generations of Black families that have come since the act was passed.

Action 38

Reroute Interstate Highways and Repair Communities

President Dwight Eisenhower initiated the interstate highway program, officially called the National Interstate and Defense Highways

Act of 1956, with the goal of building roads that linked every state in the country. This helped with travel, interstate commerce, military readiness, and access to the new, sprawling suburbs. Suburbs developed as white people began to move out of cities after Blacks came en masse from the South as political refugees fleeing Jim Crow and looking for better economic conditions. To aid whites in what has become known as "white flight," the federal government built interstate highways so that while moving farther from the city, whites could easily commute between downtown jobs and suburban neighborhoods.

While making life easier for white people, these federally funded interstate highways decimated entire enterprise zones for Blacks. The routes they chose went through Black commercial and residential districts. For this reason, in most metropolitan cities in the United States you can find a historic district for virtually all ethnicities except for African Americans because ours was destroyed during the building of the interstate highway.

It happened in cities like Nashville in 1967, where Interstate 40 curved to miss a white neighborhood and destroyed a Black one instead. In my home state of Alabama, Birmingham planners did the same thing with Interstate 59. In Los Angeles, building Interstates 5 and 10 and US Highway 101 caused the Pico and Sugar Hill neighborhoods to be leveled. And few examples are as severe or indicative of the sheer devastation and impact as what happened in Tulsa, Oklahoma.[28]

Tulsa's highway planners chose to go through the heart of the Greenwood District, the same district that was bombed in 1921, leveling 1,256 homes and leaving ten thousand people homeless in less than eighteen hours. After all of that destruction done by the deputized members of the white mob, Klan, and others, the people chose to rebuild, without ever getting an insurance check and having had their money stolen by their white banks. By the 1950s, Greenwood was bigger and better than before. All of that meant nothing to the highway planners. What they did not finish in 1921, the building of I-244 accomplished between 1957 and 1971. Sadly, Greenwood, like other large, successful Black enterprise zones, proved to be no match for the federal highway system.

In many communities, these interstate highways have become America's inner-city Berlin Wall to economic opportunity. Where one side is prosperous, the other side has little to no economic development and people live in utter poverty.

Therefore, this action calls for the Department of Transportation to study the economic impact it has caused on African Americans and make sizable investment into Black communities, to include paving streets, building sidewalks, and creating safer crossways. This action also calls for rerouting interstate highways away from historic Black enterprise zones that were bulldozed during their construction.[29] Removal of them is the first step, and restoring the Black economic ethos of those communities is the next—by rebuilding housing and businesses. Economic development must be funded and grants given to African Americans to start businesses in those districts—with priority given to those who had businesses there before the interstate was built. This process should be community driven and backed with federal dollars.

In addition, the Department of Transportation should make sure that in every highway construction job, a dedicated percentage of the contracts go to Black-owned companies.

In November 2021, President Biden signed the public works bill and Transportation Secretary Pete Buttigieg pledged to use $1 billion "to remedy racial inequities in U.S. highway design, such as roads that were built to separate predominantly minority neighborhoods from White communities."[30] He calls the initiative "Reconnecting Communities," and while not many specifics have been given, the news is a step in the right direction. This action can help shed more light on issues that need to be addressed. As President Ronald Reagan told Mikhail Gorbachev to "tear down that wall," referring to the Berlin Wall that separated East and West Berlin, we need to do the same thing in America: tear down these interstate highways that have become walls dividing communities.

Action 39

Reimburse Victims of Urban Removal

The building of the interstate highway was not the only nail in the coffin to the Black community's economic advancement during the latter half of the twentieth century. In an effort to rid communities of blight and slums, the federal government bought land and allowed private developers to build on it. America tends to view the world through the lens of white supremacy, seeing Black lives, bodies, and possessions as slum and blight—things of little value that need to be developed.

Urban renewal was so effective in destroying Black communities it was known as "Urban Removal." "Urban renewal is Negro removal" was a common refrain. Not only were the families removed, they were cheated, given far less than market value for their homes, left unable to purchase a house equal to what they had. At the same time urban renewal was happening, government housing was being built. In this process Blacks were recruited to live in these new apartment buildings that would later turn into what many refer today as the ghetto.

History professor Brent Cebul wrote, "At its peak in the mid-1960s, urban renewal displaced a minimum of 50,000 families *annually*—a 1964 House of Representatives report estimated the figure at more like 66,000. . . . While Black Americans were just 13 percent of the total population in 1960, they comprised at least 55 percent of those displaced. And, while we tend to remember urban renewal as a big-city program, pursued by titans such as Robert Moses in New York, the vast majority of projects were carried out in cities of 50,000 residents or fewer."[31] According to Dr. Mindy Fullilove, author of *Root Shock: How Tearing Up City Neighborhoods Hurts America, and What We Can Do about It*, by 1962 some eight hundred Black communities had been displaced.[32] When families are dispossessed, the political and social institutions deteriorate, and the rich community ethos evaporates.

Therefore this action calls for immediate payment to the people who were cheated by the federal government and not given fair market value for their property. In the absence of the individuals who were cheated, their descendants should receive payments. Payments can be calculated by reviewing what was paid and how far it was from fair market value, adjusting that difference for inflation and adding compounded interest for the years since the property was taken. HUD funds should be given to neighborhood associations within the Black communities impacted to help reinvigorate and stabilize the Black neighborhoods. This will help restore trust and make amends for the hardship and anguish inflicted on people who had their land taken from them for little payment.

Action 40

Repurpose the Ghettos

With redlining dictating where Blacks could live, the interstate highway becoming the walls that surrounded them, and urban renewal removing the remaining Blacks from areas that whites wanted to develop, the small area where many Blacks had to live became densely populated. The federal government, through the Department of Housing and Urban Development (HUD), constructed large, often high-rise apartment complexes to house the urban poor. HUD started under President Lyndon Johnson in 1965 as a way to fight poverty. However, with their low-grade building quality, poor management, high poverty, high crime, and limited resources allotted for things like routine trash pickup, rodent and pest management, and capital improvements, these housing projects became what is called the ghetto. By definition, a ghetto is a slum area where homogenous groups of people live. The term was first used derogatorily to describe the area where Jews were forced to reside in European cities. The segregation and persecution associated with historic ghettos is not something the United States should tolerate for any segment of its population.

Because the ghetto is a government creation, it should be the government's responsibility to create better alternatives for residents and for use of those properties. I propose reimagining and repurposing those facilities, turning the high-density family housing into transitional living communities, similar to college dormitories for low-income residents, with a resident assistant for each floor—a licensed social worker or clinician who can assist those on their floor with food, health, and job needs. Public safety is managed by social workers and the building manager lives on-site to ensure everything is working smoothly and find permanent housing for all residents. A communal kitchen in each building is staffed to provide food for those living in that building.

Imagine the campus surrounding these buildings with a gated entry to allow only residents, offices for medical screening and treatment, life coaching and mentoring, financial literacy classes, job training, day care for children and the elderly, as well as recreational activities like basketball and tennis. Resident requirements will include participation in the activities. If this cannot be done, the government should send everyone substantial amounts in vouchers to live where they can be in an environment where these amenities can be accessed within five miles.

By repurposing government housing from being a warehouse of poor people to a place where the residents can receive meaningful life skills and nutritious meals in their own safe neighborhood, we can reduce poverty and move people toward the goal of wealth-building homeownership.

Action 41

Eliminate Confederate Holidays

National appreciation for the US military is a patriotic and appropriate gesture, because, since the beginning of this nation, brave men and women have fought to make and keep it free. We have two holidays to celebrate those men and women: Veterans Day, when we recognize all who served, and Memorial Day (which was originated by African Americans in honor of the soldiers who fought for the Union), when we recognize and remember those who died in sacrifice for our freedom.

Meanwhile, some states celebrate those who killed American soldiers. Ten states—Alabama, Mississippi, Arkansas, Georgia, Florida, Kentucky, North Carolina, South Carolina, Tennessee, and Texas—still have official state holidays celebrating Confederate soldiers. Alabama and Mississippi each have three such holidays: Robert E. Lee Day (on the same day as Martin Luther King Jr. Day), Confederate Memorial Day, and Jefferson Davis's birthday. Georgia has a state law mandating the governor establish one day recognizing the Confederacy, though since 2015 the former Robert E. Lee Day and Confederate Memorial Day are simply called "State Holiday" on the official calendar.[33] Tennessee honors Confederate general and former Grand Wizard of the Ku Klux Klan Nathan Bedford Forrest.

Confederate soldiers were traitors who supported secession from the United States of America and killed hundreds of thousands of US soldiers. To honor them is a gross gesture of disrespect to all the brave people who fought and died in the Civil War fighting for the preservation of the United States; it is disrespectful to their descendants, and it is disdainful to the descendants of the people those Confederates were fighting to keep enslaved.

Therefore this action calls for the elimination of all such Confederate holidays, many of which were put into place to protest the federal government making Rev. Dr. Martin Luther King's birthday a national holiday. No wonder it's hard for some to want to repair the harm caused by slavery and racial terror, when they live in states still celebrating the perpetrators of those horrors and subsidizing their memorials (see actions 15 and 16). Where these are paid holidays for state workers, they cost the state money that could be utilized to support more reparatory programs such as education about the Civil War's cost, consequences, and treasonous traitors.

Action 42

Support Black Veterans

In 1944, Congress passed the Servicemen's Readjustment Act, commonly known as the GI Bill. It provided benefits to veterans such as unemployment insurance, college tuition, and low-interest home loans. The GI Bill was transformational for those who accessed its benefits, which—not surprisingly—was primarily white veterans. As a result, "the wide disparity in the bill's implementation ended up helping drive growing gaps in wealth, education and civil rights between white and Black Americans."[34]

More than one million Black veterans valiantly fought in segregated ranks, survived under the worst of conditions, and helped defeat Nazi Germany, only to return to Jim Crow racist America whose eyes could not see Black patriots, only Black problems. Therefore, these patriots did not receive the same benefits that white veterans enjoyed. With the same tactics utilized with the implementation of the New Deal, southern Democrats wrote into the bill that the funds had to be administered by the states, knowing full well that southern states would not distribute much, if anything, to Black veterans.

Several other impediments were codified into the bill. One was not allowing veterans with dishonorable discharges to receive any benefits; Black soldiers receive dishonorable discharges at a much higher rate than their white counterparts. For those Black soldiers who did qualify, it was difficult to find places that would honor their benefits. Segregated colleges would not allow them to be admitted even with the government paying the tuition. Redlining and restrictive neighborhood covenants made it hard for Black veterans to buy houses, even with the low-cost home loans promised by the bill. In some cases, postmasters simply did not deliver the mail containing applications for unemployment benefits to Black veterans.[35]

Hence action 34 calls on the Department of Veterans Affairs to identify World War II Black veterans and compensate their descendants with what they were due upon returning to the country they risked their lives for. Payment should include adjustments for inflation for their unemployment, college tuition, home loans, and everything else they were entitled to as veterans. Imagine where these veterans' descendants would be today if they'd been able to earn the higher pay that often comes with a college degree or build the equity that comes through homeownership. The model is there. We have seen how well the GI Bill worked for some; now it is incumbent that we ensure it works for all.

Action 43

Rectify Injustice in the Department of Veterans Affairs

Having as its mission "to care for those who have served in our nation's military and for their families, caregivers and survivors," the Department of Veterans Affairs (VA) has fallen far short in its treatment of Black servicemen and women as well as Black employees, some of whom also happen to be veterans.

As discussed above, the VA discriminated against Blacks in the administration of the GI Bill.

Recently a Freedom of Information Act request by the National Veterans Council for Legal Redress and the Black Veterans Project revealed that according to VA records, "the average denial rate for disability compensation was 5.3% higher for Black veterans than their white counterparts between 2001 and 2020. And the racial disparity for average acceptance rates was even higher—6.8%."[36]

In late 2022, the Yale Law School's Veterans Legal Services Clinic filed a lawsuit in federal court alleging, "The results of VA's racial discrimination has been to deny countless meritorious applications by Black veterans, depriving them and their families of care and support that their faithful service has earned." For its part, the VA has acknowledged the "unacceptable disparities in both VA benefits decisions and military discharge status due to racism," but says it needs to do more study of the role race played.[37]

The VA has also received complaints from its employees. In August 2020, the American Federation of Government Employees (AFGE), a union whose members include VA employees, announced that 78 percent of VA employees surveyed feel racism is a "moderate to serious" problem within the department. The VA secretary at that time, Donald Trump appointee Robert Wilkie, was a member of the Sons of Confederate Veterans and fostered an atmosphere of ambivalence at best and hostility at worse for the department's Black employees.[38]

As a result of the survey, Alma Lee, president of the AFGE National VA Council, wrote a letter making recommendations to the secretary, which I wholeheartedly agree with and adopt as some of my suggested actions for this department:

1. "Acknowledge that racism and discrimination is widespread at VA facilities nationwide."
2. "Withdraw the contract proposal to ban staff representation in EEO interviews."

3. "Affirm that all VA workplaces must be free from bigotry, harassment, and retaliation, and take the appropriate steps to ensure that these basic rights are upheld."
4. "Meet with AFGE leadership to discuss best practices and next steps in combating racism at the VA."[39]

President Biden signed a bill in November 2021 requiring the Governmental Accountability Office to investigate whether racism was at play in the decision making at the VA.[40]

In addition to these actions, compensation should be made to the families who have collectively lost over a trillion dollars in benefits. Since many of the Black veterans died before receiving their benefit, this action calls for their lost benefits to be adjusted for inflation and go to their nearest kin. VA hospitals that have closed in predominantly Black towns should be reopened, and new ones opened where needed in order to better serve Black veterans. Let's truly fulfill the mission of caring for the families of veterans and pass down the benefits denied Black veterans to their children and grandchildren.

Action 44

Increase Promotion and Recognition of Blacks in the Military

I grew up hearing that "there is no place for a Black man in the white man's military." I most often have heard this from Black veterans as they recount their time in service. Sadly, this appears to be true, according to a 2020 analysis of the military community that reported 90 percent of the generals are white, and Blacks "make up 9 percent of active-duty officers but only 6.5 percent of generals."[41]

Besides being paid significantly more, generals create strategy. In the past, these strategies created segregated regiments with white men as their leaders. These strategies sent Black soldiers to the worst parts of the battle and placed them on the front line. Diversifying the generals will also aid the military as a whole, given that "research shows that racially diverse groups tend to be more innovative and creative, that diversity can strengthen civil-military relations, and that morale among rank-and-file African Americans would probably benefit from more equal representation in the most visible and iconic positions in the U.S. armed forces."[42]

In light of the rich history of African Americans fighting in every US war, though that is largely unknown to the common citizen, there ought to be a space in the orientation of soldiers to highlight the contribution of Black soldiers. From the first person to die for the new democracy we call the United States, Crispus Attucks, and Blacks fighting in the Civil War (including Harriet Tubman, who served as a spy and scout), to more modern examples including the Buffalo Soldiers, Harlem Hellfighters, and Tuskegee Airmen—so many Black soldiers have served our country in spite of its failure to provide them justice. Knowing all of American military history is important for all military personnel. A more informed soldier is a better soldier.

Action 45

Diversify Military Contracts

In addition to diversifying the military's officer corps, we must diversify military contract recipients. Blacks should at least get their portion of the military contracts. The largest expenditure in the US budget is for defense—$743 billion in 2022. It would go a long way in repairing the harm of racism both within the military and outside if some of those contracts were given to Black-owned companies in proportion to their military service.

Blacks make up 16.8 percent of the military,[43] but little is known about how much in contracts they receive from the Department of Defense. "Analysis of the federal contracting landscape shows that minority-owned and women-owned businesses are getting a pittance in terms of contracting opportunities." In fiscal year 2020, $560 billion of the $650 billion spent on federal contracts for goods and services could have gone to small businesses; however, "minority-owned small businesses received just 9.4% of those small-business eligible federal contracting dollars and women-owned small businesses a mere 4.9%. To put this into perspective, almost 19% of US employer businesses are minority-owned and just under 21% are owned by women."[44]

This action calls on the government to collect and report the data of how much Department of Defense spending goes to Black-owned companies. This action complements President Biden's Executive Order 13985, which calls for Equity Action Plans in order to advance an equity and racial justice initiative. The results and findings of this plan should include the number and amount of contracts to Black-owned businesses, and the information should be shared with the public and historically Black organizations.

Action 46

Strike the Punishment Clause from the Thirteenth Amendment

The Thirteenth Amendment reads, "Neither slavery nor involuntary servitude, *except as a punishment for crime whereof the party shall have been duly convicted,* shall exist within the United States, or any place subject to their jurisdiction" (emphasis mine). Action 46 calls for this exception to be stricken from the Thirteenth Amendment. This clause undermines the true intent of the amendment and creates a loophole that permits slavery to continue. It enables the racist approach to policing and prosecution of crimes that began after emancipation and continues today.

The history of policing in America began with the slave patrols, with the goal of catching runaway enslaved people, and evolved after emancipation to enforce the black codes—especially vagrancy laws that made it illegal for Blacks to not have a job (when the main type of employment available to Black men was sharecropping). Those who were arrested were leased out to work for landowners and businesses. The inmates were paid nothing—a system through which whites regained the free labor source they'd lost at emancipation.

Douglas Blackmon articulates the horrors of convict leasing in his 2008 book *Slavery by Another Name.* Children as young as ten or eleven were arrested. Inmates were sent to work at places like the Chattahoochee Brick Company, in a facility so hot that the guards would not bring their guns for fear that the heat would cause them to discharge. Like enslaved people of antebellum times, incarcerated workers could be whipped and abused, robbed of their humanity.

Convict leasing in the late nineteenth and early twentieth centuries began the incestuous relationship between privatized prisons and profits that we see today, when prison companies are traded on the stock market. Rather than sending jobs overseas to pay factory workers pennies, American manufacturers contract with prisons as a cheap domestic labor source, enriching corporate executives while paying incarcerated workers far less than minimum wage.

The incarcerated are still citizens; being convicted of a felony does not mean you are any less human nor less of an American. A person can be sentenced for a crime and be confined to a location, a cell, for a set number of years, but they should never lose their humanity. Action 46 calls on Congress to act to strike this clause from the Constitution and encourages the people of the United States to ratify this change and make slavery in all its forms illegal once and for all.

Action 47

Expunge Felony Records for Nonviolent Crimes

According to Dr. Khalid Muhammad, national chairman of the New Black Panther Party at the time of his death in 2001, in my home state of Alabama, in the 1850s some 99 percent of people incarcerated were white, while in the 1880s some 85 percent of people incarcerated were Black. These numbers reflect how mass incarceration began for Blacks immediately after emancipation from slavery. Today the incarceration rate for Blacks continues to exceed their number in the general population. Blacks make up roughly 13 percent of the population but 38 percent of the US prison population.[45]

The pivot that occurred once Blacks were freed from chattel slavery is obvious—they were marked as wards of the state, stripped whenever possible of their freedom and humanity through our judicial system. Dehumanization does not end when a person is released from prison. Convicted felons are not able to receive student loans or government housing, are prohibited from owning a gun, are unable to get a professional license, and often have great trouble finding a job.

Felony expungements for nonviolent crimes should be automatic and should occur immediately after someone is cleared of wrongdoing or released from prison, put on parole, or given probation. Currently, in most states there is a multiyear waiting period during which being labeled as a felon prevents a person from fully integrating back into society, which makes recidivism more likely, perpetuating the cycle.

People have fallen prey to a society that failed them, becoming what we made them to be. We often see the incarcerated as the predators, but we have also failed them, especially nonviolent offenders. For too long we have "locked them up and thrown away the key," and even when they are released, we treat them as less human, less American.

Action 48

Restore Voting Rights

The next action will ensure that people will not lose their right to vote because they have been convicted of a crime. Inmates are counted in census (therefore gaining representation for the surrounding community) and utilized to work to bring massive profit to corporate America, but they are not allowed to vote while incarcerated, and they remain disenfranchised after release.

It is embarrassingly sad that in the first modern democracy, we take voting rights away from those who have been convicted of a crime. One of the hallmarks of a democracy is allowing citizens over a certain age to vote. Passing a character test should not be a requirement for voting, but unfortunately in America it is. Having a criminal record is akin to failing a character test, which now has prevented countless voters from being enfranchised—just like the poll tax, grandfather clause, and other arbitrary and capricious tests used to deny Blacks the right to vote before the 1965 Voting Rights Act.

In most states, released inmates have to go through much red tape to reapply, a process that takes years and is so onerous most do not bother to go through it. Therefore, not taking away their right to vote to begin with would be very beneficial for us as a nation to ensure we do not deny anyone the right to participate in the democratic process. Having the right to vote did not cause them to commit a crime, and taking that right from them will not help them become a better citizen, but it does hurt our democracy to not hear their voice. Therefore, this action calls on voting rights and voting access to not be lost for a person convicted of a felony.

Action 49

Ban the Box

Another penalty that comes with being a convicted felon is having to disclose that record by checking a certain box on every job application. Thus action 49 calls on the US Equal Employment Opportunity Commission (EEOC) to make it illegal for employers—including the federal government—to put this question on a job application. This box has been used to deny employment to Blacks who meet the qualifications but have a criminal record. If an applicant meets the requirements and if the employer feels they can do the job well, a criminal record should not matter to their application.

Now, this action does not call for the elimination of criminal background checks, which are important in the fields of education and child care. It simply allows applicants a fair shot at getting an interview, rather than allowing employers to rule out applicants based on their criminal history before even meeting them. It is apparent how skewed our criminal justice system has been, especially as it relates to Blacks; therefore the goal of this action is to help employers get to meet the actual person, to increase their chances of being seen as human and gaining employment.

Gainful employment is necessary in reducing the enticement of a return to crime. Today, legislatures in more than twenty states have voted to "ban the box"; this action calls on all of them to do so.

Action 50

Stop Asset Forfeiture

Asset forfeiture, the confiscation of goods and funds perceived as having enabled crime or been the profit of crime, is fraught with corruption. Police might keep the items they confiscate, even holding contests to see who can acquire the most. District attorneys often wait at least a year and often after the statute of limitations has run out to file the forfeiture, and then the individuals who had their assets taken have thirty days to claim them and must show that they obtained them legally. Most significantly for our purposes, the system unfairly targets Black men.

The Equal Justice Initiative reported, "An investigation by the *Greenville News* found that South Carolina police are systematically seizing millions of dollars each year in cash and property—often from people who are not guilty of a crime and disproportionately from Black men. . . . Black men . . . comprise 13 percent of South Carolina's population, but make up 65 percent of those targeted for civil forfeiture. White people are twice as likely as Black people to get their money back."[46]

According to Justice Ruth Bader Ginsburg in her majority opinion in *Timbs v. Indiana* (2019), asset forfeiture is a relic of the convict leasing system. It also finds its roots in the black codes where laws against such "dubious offenses" as vagrancy were used to arrest Blacks, levy "draconian fines," and then demand "involuntary labor" when the fines could not be paid.[47]

To correct this injustice, actions need to be taken—as they have in some states—to use asset forfeiture only when there is a criminal conviction, and the money taken must be given to a nonprofit in the same zip code that focuses on youth education or adult job training. Such donations serve the community and prevent future crime.

Action 51

Create a Business Pathway for Marijuana Dealers

One of the biggest issues for recently released inmates is that they have little to no marketable job skills. Even after the "box" is banned (see action 49), that obstacle to employment remains. However, with the marijuana industry, it is different. Today we have over forty thousand people with job training and skills to sell and use marijuana who are still incarcerated.[48] Action 51 calls for the justice system to release those incarcerated on marijuana-related charges, expunge their records, and allow them to own or sell to cannabis dispensaries.

Our economy is missing out on their knowledge and expertise and all the enhancements they can bring to the emerging cannabis industry. According to DISA Global Solutions, a company that does drug testing and background checks, as of this writing there are more than twenty states where marijuana is fully legal and four where it is completely illegal—Idaho, Kansas, South Carolina, and Wyoming. In the rest, marijuana is either legal as CBD with THC, legal for medicinal purposes, or at least decriminalized.[49] Yet there are still more than forty thousand people incarcerated in America today on marijuana charges.

After all the harm the so-called war on drugs did to Black communities all over America—arresting so many Black men for selling or using marijuana—the sale of marijuana and its oils is now being permitted and many people (largely not Black) are legally benefiting from the same thing that got these men arrested. Action 51 calls for the immediate release of all those incarcerated on marijuana-related charges in states where marijuana or its oils are now legal, and it also calls for those recently released to be given preference and start-up capital for creating their own cannabis business.

Action 52

Continue Pandemic-Era Decarceration

Since incarceration was the first place newly freed enslaved people were shipped en masse after emancipation, in order to fully repair one of the lasting vestiges of slavery and white supremacy, we need to eradicate or highly modify America's prison system. Complete abolishment of prisons is advocated by those who identify with the "defund the police" movement. They have grown skeptical of reforming a system that has been used since 1865 to subjugate Blacks in "slavery by another name." Prison abolitionists seek to reroute funds for policing to social service programs like homelessness, mental health, job training, and so on. (See action 53.)

The Brookings Institution has proposed three types of prison reforms aimed at helping to reduce recidivism, acclimate the freed inmates to civilian life, and build up the inmates, who for the most part come from a highly vulnerable part of our society. The approaches are divided into short-, middle-, and long-term goals. Brookings's short-term reform proposal builds on positive action that was taken during the COVID-19 pandemic.[50]

During the pandemic, many states released a number of prisoners (convicted of nonviolent and nonsexual offences) and gave alternative sentences. Many older prisoners and those with health concerns were given early release. While prison populations remained high, these efforts were done to reduce the spread of COVID-19 in the prison population and especially to protect those with health conditions that increased their risk from the virus. Democratic- and Republican-led states joined in this effort, and there was no notable uptick in crime as a result of the releases, proving that these actions should continue as part of a more just era in prison reform.

Action 53

Focus on Rehabilitation in Prison

Another step in the prison reform movement is to keep the prison system but to treat the inmates like people, from the moment of arrest to their release. Consider the cases of Freddie Gray, who died, and Randy Cox, who became paralyzed from the neck down, as a result of how police transported them after their arrests.

Brookings's medium- and long-term suggestions for criminal justice reform include pretrial diversion programs, alternative dispute resolution programs, and alternative sentencing initiatives, which give more discretion to the judge in sentencing options.[51] Restorative approaches to justice include things like victim offender mediation, conferencing (includes more than just the victim and offender), circling (which include trained facilitators), community panels and boards, victim surrogate programs, and truth and reconciliation commissions. For those given a prison sentence, we should be encouraging a rehabilitative focus, including training in anger management, conflict resolution, self-improvement, work-force development, and vocational training.

Robert Martinson's 1974 report on prison reform concluded that "nothing works" in prison.[52] Sadly, much of what happens in prisons today is archaic, still solely focused on punishment and not based on current best practices for improved outcomes. State legislators should implement rehabilitation-focused prison reform for all state prisons, and Congress should do the same for the federal prisons, prioritizing job training and character development. Studies show that when inmates learn a job skill while incarcerated, they are less likely to commit crime again. Norway has a done an exceptional job of this. America should study and apply it to our prison system.[53]

Action 54

End Mandatory Sentencing

Our prisons are absurdly overcrowded, and racism runs rampant in every sector of our criminal justice system.[54] Mandatory minimums in sentencing compound both problems and undermine democratic election. Even in municipalities where African Americans are in the majority and have elected judges who may be more sympathetic to defendants, judges have virtually no discretion in sentencing under mandatory sentencing statutes.

Mandatory sentencing began shortly after the 1965 Voting Rights bill passed, when Congress and state legislatures across the country began to pass bills eliminating the autonomy of judges elected by the people (who then included more Black voters). "Beginning in the mid-1970s, Congress began to lengthen sentences, culminating in the 1984 Comprehensive Crime Control Act, which established mandatory minimum sentences and eliminated federal parole."[55] Later, mandatory minimums were applied to drug sentences by the Anti-Drug Abuse Act of 1986, then in 1988 a five-year mandatory minimum was set for simple possession of crack cocaine. The Violent Crime Control and Law Enforcement Act of 1994 created a three-strikes provision at the federal level. So now, at a federal level and in more than half of the states, if you have two prior fel-onies, the third requires a sentence of life in prison.[56]

Ending mandatory sentences would return the discretion to ensure the person convicted is given an appropriate sentence to those who know their case the best—the judge and jury who have heard the facts of each individual case.

Action 55

Ensure Fair Jury Selection

Speaking of juries, for the majority of American history, juries have been predominantly white, as have the prosecutors and judges. The Sixth Amendment to the Constitution guarantees that "in all crimi-nal prosecutions, the accused shall enjoy the right to a speedy and public trial, by an impartial jury of the State and district wherein the crime shall have been committed."

For African Americans, for the majority of their time in this country they have not been able to receive an impartial jury. It was only in 1986 that the Supreme Court decided that "the use of peremptory challenges to remove a potential juror from the jury pool based on race violates the Equal Protection Clause of the Four-teenth Amendment to the Constitution."[57] However, Black jurors can still be struck as long as the reason is not explicitly because they are Black. This subjective process has continued to allow all-white juries for Black defendants all over the country. According to the research of the Equal Justice Initiative, "Black people are under-represented in prosecutors' offices and in the judiciary. More than 40% of Americans are people of color, but 95% of elected prose-cutors are white. Similar disparities exist within the judiciary."[58]

Most states have laws saying the jury pool should be identical to the representation in the overall population, but judges (the over-whelming majority of whom are white) "routinely fail to enforce these requirements."[59]

To address this, we must (1) review all cases of Black prisoners who were found guilty by all-white juries; (2) establish positions for racial monitoring to ensure that jury pools match the population and mandate that not just the jury pool but the jury itself should reflect the population; and (3) require that for every case involving a Black defendant and a white prosecutor and judge, there is at least one Black person on the jury.

Until this is put in place, for every case where there is an all-white jury, courts should send a notice to community organizations who advocate for social justice issues like the NAACP and predominantly Black churches to inform them of the date of the trials to promote community oversight.

Action 56

Require Racial Impact Study in Police Departments

In light of the disproportionate number of Black Americans arrested and incarcerated, we must put policies in place to ensure that law enforcement does its work without racial bias. A first step toward this goal is to require retroactive study of policing based on race. Each state attorney general's office should have a division of civil rights and hire third-party analysts to critically examine use of force, police stops, places monitored, hiring practices, and cross-racial neighborhood complaints.

Recent laws requiring "racial impact statements" are a step toward the Sentencing Project's call for "states to adopt forecasting estimates that will calculate the impact of proposed crime legislation on different populations in order to minimize or eliminate the racially disparate impacts of certain laws and policies." The project also correctly states that "the impact of racial impact laws will be modest at best if they remain only forward looking."[60]

For this reason, analysis of racial impact in policing must also be retrospective. Because we know justice has not been blind in this country on a federal, state, or local level, we should work to ensure that those convicted of crimes are actually guilty and not a victim of racist criminal justice practice (i.e., all-white jury, police misconduct, forced testimony, poor defense, overzealous district attorney, or a judge with a history of being harsh on Black defendants). The work of nonprofits such as the Innocence Project should be institutionalized, seeking to make sure the people in prison are actually guilty and have not suffered from a wrongful conviction.

The goal of racial impact studies is to find where any errors occurred, be vigilant in resolving them, and discover methods of crime prevention that are proactive in preventing discrimination, especially as it relates to Blacks.

Action 57

Adopt an Interdisciplinary Approach to Crime Prevention

There are more ways to fight crime than by arresting the suspected perpetrator. A sentient society is one in which, due to the high consciousness of the populace, police should rarely be the first responders for the complex, emotionally charged 911 calls to which mental health professional or relationship coaches would be better suited to respond.

On average, police do not prevent crime; they at best stop crime. The Marshall Project asked almost 2,400 inmates what could have kept them from being incarcerated.[61] None of their answers involved more police, greater law enforcement, or tougher sentences. All those actions are punitive and may invoke fear, but most inmates were not intimidated by fear when they got arrested. They already lived in fear. Their neighborhoods were akin to war zones, and home typically offered no refuge from the fear and anxiety of the streets.

Prior to being arrested, fear of being killed or robbed was a ubiquitous threat that lingered at every corner and over every meal. Asking them what could have helped keep them out of prison, their responses included mental health care, drug treatment programs, affordable housing, living-wage jobs, better education, job training, domestic violence prevention, and transportation. What drove them to crime was not a lack of fear but a lack of resources.

Fear is what those who are afraid of criminals want them to have; it goes back to the whole eye-for-an-eye approach. You make me afraid, so I want to use the police to make you afraid. This happens even when there is no real threat of bodily harm. For some police, just the sight of Black men and even boys like Tamir Rice causes officers to fear for their life and shoot to kill. When Terrence Crutcher was shot and killed in Tulsa, the police officers could be heard saying he looks like a "bad dude" right before he was shot and killed. It's not just the police who are afraid of Blacks; we also see the alarming rate at which white women call the police on Blacks for the most innocuous actions: being at a park, using an elevator where they live, going for a walk. These white women are afraid of Black people and want them to leave, and if they refuse, they call the police, hoping that action will invoke the same fear in the Blacks that the white person feels. White fear should be addressed with unconscious bias training—not more policing.

A more interdisciplinary approach to policing would both prevent crime and reduce the types of interactions that result in unnecessary police involvement. In far too many cities, the largest budget item is the police department, and yet crime has not been reduced much. Having a multidimensional approach removes people from the situation that caused them to lead lives of criminal activity. An office of crime prevention should be established to oversee this interdisciplinary approach for all communities and zip codes, with a special priority on predominantly Black areas. Additionally, Congress should make receiving federal dollars contingent upon implementing an interdisciplinarian approach to law enforcement.

Action 58

Partner with Communities to Prevent Gun Violence

The Bureau of Alcohol, Tobacco, Firearms and Explosives (ATF) in the Justice Department must keep track of the race and ethnicity of gun owners and diligently remove illegal firearms through government buy-back programs, utilizing partnerships that are led by people from the communities in which they make most of their arrests. The ATF agents should not come into Black communities simply to make arrests but to make partnerships.

The ATF should ensure that the zip codes where crimes are committed receive the money meant to reduce crime. The statistics on crime and best practices to avoid them should be shared with the communities that see the crime on a regular basis. The office should partner with local grassroots nonprofits such as We Our Us in Baltimore, Maryland, which aims to eliminate violence in the inner city by establishing partnerships with and hiring community leaders and by holding weekly rallies, food distributions, workshops, peace walks, and job placement opportunities on a regular basis.

Action 59

Establish Universal Pre-K / Head Start

Not many areas discussed in this book have as deep and long a history of racial animus toward Blacks as the education system in the United States. As we will discuss over the next few action steps, this country has denied African Americans the right to learn from the moment we arrived on these shores, in increasingly creative ways over the centuries. During slavery, it was against the law for the enslaved to know how to read or write. Immediately after slavery, Blacks formed schools to educate themselves. These schools were often housed in churches and were burned repeatedly by the Ku Klux Klan. Even after public schools were formed, Black children were forced to attend underfunded, segregated schools. Colleges and universities had to be formed as well because the government prohibited Blacks from attending white colleges. The public white schools and colleges received government funding while the Black schools received very little and had outdated supplies, overcrowded classrooms, and underpaid teachers.

This abhorrent act of reckless neglect for a significant segment of the population does not impact merely those generations in yesteryear but also current and future ones. Seeing as how parents, grandparents, and caregivers are the first teachers of babies, the impact of poor education trickles down and must be remedied at all levels, starting with children's formative years.

This action calls for free universal pre-kindergarten or Head Start for all Black children beginning at age three. Currently Head Start is available for children ages three to five from families with income below the poverty line, a criterion that could be expanded to give all Black children the foundational education their ancestors often lacked. Many people have advocated for universal pre-kindergarten in recent years, and some states have implemented the policy allowing any family to enroll their four- or five-year-old child.[62] This policy must be implemented nationwide. Providing free early childhood education for Black children helps repair the damage of undereducating their parents, grandparents, and great-grandparents.

Action 60

Increase Funding for Majority-Black Public Schools

In the segregated public school system that dominated the United States for at least one hundred years, Black schools were never top priority. Black schools got the discarded books, desks, office supplies, and equipment of the white schools. Black children had to walk to school, bring their own lunch, purchase their books and, of course, their own supplies. Black families who were already overworked and underpaid had to pay taxes for a public school system that failed them and their children by not distributing resources equally.

Because of the poor funding, Black children had to attend school in buildings that were in grave need of repair, crowd into classrooms (sometimes with multiple grade levels in one room), be taught by underpaid teachers compared to their white counterparts. As for the curriculum, some topics were left out—like civil rights guaranteed in the Constitution's Bill of Rights and any talk of liberation and equality highlighted in the Declaration of Independence.[63] (Current bans on anything labeled "critical race theory" seem similarly motivated.)

Today there is still a difference between predominantly Black and white schools. According to the Century Foundation, the funding gap for majority Black or Latino school districts is, on average, more than $5,000 per student. This gap is "defined as the amount of money needed to bring students to the national average performance, as measured by test scores. . . . The formula assumes that more money is needed for places with large numbers of children in poverty, with disabilities and who are learning English. It also takes into account the cost of living, teacher wages and the size of the district to account for economies of scale."[64]

Even more sadly, nearly seventy years after *Brown v. Board of Education*, schools are more segregated today than they were in the 1960s.[65] "In 1968, 77% of Black students across the nation attended majority nonwhite schools. . . . That sank to 63% in the 1980s, but rose to 81% in 2018."[66]

This resegregation of schools is the result of several factors. First of all, enforcement of *Brown v. Board of Education* focused primarily on states that had Jim Crow laws, which were typically but not all in the South. Immediately following enforcement of *Brown*, many whites with financial means moved out of school districts with large Black populations or created private schools and academies, leaving public schools primarily to the Black students. While government-sanctioned segregation was outlawed with *Brown*, modern residential segregation flourished, and neighborhood schools became the new goal.

Schools are often funded by the property taxes of the surrounding neighborhoods. The majority of Blacks attend schools in the inner city, where corporations, factories, plants, highways, and absentee landlords—all of which depress property value—dominate. Add that Black homes, due to racism, have historically been appraised and assessed at a lower value than whites', and this system puts Black students at an even greater disadvantage.

Poor funding leads to fewer teachers, resources, extracurricular activities, arts, STEM programs, and more. The results are overcrowded classrooms, less instruction time, less well-rounded students, and shorter resumes, all of which makes it more difficult to get into college, let alone receive a much-needed scholarship. In the age of standardized testing, many districts award more funds to high-performing schools, when it should be the other way around.

To remedy this historic wrong, this action calls on Congress and state legislatures to increase funds for schools with an African American enrollment greater than 51 percent. These funds should go to support services including transportation, counseling, after-school tutorial programs for all subjects and for college prep courses, as well as for the arts, STEM, athletic programs, libraries, and facility improvements. Last but absolutely not least, teachers at schools that are over 51 percent Black should receive additional pay.

Action 61

End Racist Educational Tracking and Discipline Policies

While the *Brown v. Board of Education* Supreme Court ruling happened in 1954, it took school systems across the country and especially in the South around sixteen years to fully integrate schools.[67] Some school systems closed for an entire year instead of integrating. (Consider what that says about white parents' priorities when they would *not* close schools even in response to the COVID-19 pandemic.) Klansman and Senator Robert Byrd, along with one hundred other congressmen, signed the "Southern Manifesto," vowing to fight integration through such methods as pupil placement boards, tuition grants, or school vouchers. The movement to defund and dismantle public schools that began then still exists today.[68]

Integration was a hard-fought battle. Children trying only to attend school faced verbal harassment and physical assault. Parents of children who integrated schools faced backlash at their jobs. When school busing was implemented as a tool for integration, white mobs violently attacked these buses and the children in them. Despite all the devious tactics described in this and the previous action, by the mid-1970s and 1980s, integrated schools were largely accepted. Within these schools, however, a variety of policies and programs kept Black students at a disadvantage.

For those schools that still had a mixture of Black and white students, schools began implementing policies like honors or advanced placement tracking, where whites far outnumbered Blacks. Special education and individual education plans (IEP) emerged and became a mechanism to categorize Black children, especially boys, as learning disabled. Dress codes restricting dress and hairstyles became ways to target Black youth. Zero-tolerance discipline policies, which have been used to suspend disproportionately Black students, created what has become known as the school-to-prison pipeline.

In Virginia the problem has been especially pronounced. It was closely studied by the Commonwealth Institute (TCI). "While Brown v. Board may be thought of as the end of schooling segregation, the truth is that we are in another chapter in the fight against it," said Ashley Kenneth, TCI senior vice president. "It is going to take a system of intentional, actionable, and anti-racist policies to make high-quality, meaningfully diverse schools a reality for more than some."[69]

Virginia Commonwealth University, which also studied segregation in Virginia schools, developed a list of recommendations that I believe should be implemented on a national level, things like establishing a reparatory justice committee in the Department of Education "to support voluntary integration and reduce segregation within and among schools"; establishing federal "certification requirements for superintendents, school boards, principals and teachers related to school segregation and integration"; collecting data on "racial, ethnic and economic school segregation"; and increasing "school board capacity to address segregation as part of rezoning."[70]

I would add that there must be disciplinary reform in schools, including a moratorium on expelling children from school except in cases of murder, rape, grave injury to a person, or physical attack on an educator. Likewise, tracking reform should include reviewing the number of Blacks placed under IEP or categorized as having a learning disability and the ethnicity of students in advanced placement courses.

Last, there should be a national apology to the Black children and their families enumerating the racist treatment of them by the education community in the United States.

Action 62

Fund HBCUs

Quakers in the North started postsecondary schools for Blacks even before emancipation. The first was Cheyney University, in 1837, followed by Lincoln University in 1854. The first college started by

Black people for Black people was Wilberforce University, established in 1856 by the African Methodist Episcopal Church. Historically Black Colleges and Universities (HBCUs) were at first largely private, though a few were financially supported by the state. Those that were funded by the state were, like their secondary and elementary counterparts, grossly underfunded. Mostly white-dominated legislatures refused to support Black colleges at the same level as they did for whites, and there were few to no Black alumni in these legislatures to advocate for their schools. Data from 1987 (the first year it could be obtained) shows that "compared to their predominantly white counterparts, the nation's Black land-grant universities have been underfunded by at least $12.8 billion over the last three decades."[71] Schools formed out of necessity due to the restraints of Jim Crow could be starved out of existence.

The United States must equalize the funding to HBCUs to make up for what they are not receiving from the states, and establish a council of Black college presidents by region to recommend how the accrediting process can be more sensitive to the needs of HBCUs. This funding would help HBCUs allocate more funds for academic support, facilities, and research.

Action 63

Offer Free College and Loan Forgiveness for Black Students

Given the refusal of most universities to admit Black students and the nation's lack of support for schools founded by and for Blacks—not to mention how the poor economic conditions in most Black communities required young people to help support their families rather than pursuing higher education—Black people have attained college degrees at a much lower rate than their counterparts of other races.

This action calls for states to provide full college scholarships to Blacks to attend any state school in the nation or any private school to which they are admitted. For Blacks who have already attended and paid for college, any and all student loan debt incurred should be forgiven.

Blacks at these schools should also receive free books and room and board because Black students historically received second-hand books and could not eat nor room with white students. And the HBCUs should receive double funding for each Black student to make up for the years when they were underfunded.

Action 64

Reaffirm Affirmative Action

In June 2023, during the writing of this book, the Supreme Court ruled that race cannot be used as a variable in college admissions. I adamantly disagree with such a decision. This action calls on Congress to codify affirmative action in college admissions to help ensure opportunities for historically oppressed Americans, especially those who have previously been systematically excluded from government-funded institutions.

While the debate over affirmative action focused on Blacks, the largest beneficiaries of affirmative action have been white women.[72] Therefore Congress should now revive affirmative action for Blacks only. This legislation could include several action items of repair found elsewhere in this book.

In 1787, Blacks were seen as only three-fifths human by the government; today, they are not seen at all by the government. This action calls on Congress to help America see us better.

Action 65

Pay College Athletes

Black athletes, male and female, are heavily involved with collegiate sports, bringing in millions of dollars of revenue for their universities but not getting paid. The *NCAA v. Alston* Supreme Court decision of 2021 unanimously approved a lower court's decision that NCAA restrictions on "education-related benefits" for college athletes violated antitrust law, but the larger, more equitable pay-for-play issue was not addressed. Even conservative Justice Brett

Kavanaugh wrote, "Nowhere else in America can businesses get away with agreeing not to pay their workers a fair market rate on the theory that their product is defined by not paying their workers a fair market rate. . . . The NCAA is not above the law."[73]

The Justice Department's Antitrust Division should investigate and file charges against the NCAA for violating their workers' rights by not paying them. All athletes play, or work, for the school, but only a select few get a contract from outside companies who seek to use their name, image, and likeness. All student athletes who play in revenue-generating sports should receive some sort of pay commensurate to how much money their sport brings to the school.

Action 66

Eliminate Debt

While America owed those it had enslaved a great debt, instead, Blacks were put in debt immediately upon release from slavery. In the South, the government returned land to the plantation owners and leaders of the Confederacy, and the newly freed enslaved people—with no property, no education, and nowhere to go—were forced back onto the plantation, given their same meager quarters in which to live and seeds to plant. Unbeknownst to them were the exorbitant fees associated with all they were "given" to utilize. Though now working for meager pay, they were largely working to pay off the debt incurred by utilizing the same things they did when they were enslaved. The former slave master became their "employer" who set both the fees and their wages. Of course, most of these transactions were done in writing while the majority of Blacks could not read nor write, so sharecroppers were highly exploited and kept as virtual enslaved people intentionally by the use of debt.

Later, as Blacks started to leave the plantations and move into cities, they fell prey to contract buying, a system in which property owners refused to sell homes to Blacks outright, regardless of their creditworthiness. Black buyers paid a substantial deposit and made monthly payments at grossly high interest rates while obtaining no equity; the title was not given until the home was paid in full.

All the while, the contract seller kept the deed and could evict the buyer at any time. No laws or regulations protected the buyers.[74]

These predatory lending practices are seen today in the title loan industry and even through banks, where Blacks often are charged higher interest rates for the same loan.

Therefore action 66 asks the United States to forgive any and all government debt or government-backed debt, including mortgages, student loans, and IRS debts, owed by African Americans and asks for the Consumer Financial Protection Bureau to mandate that credit scores of Blacks do not incorporate their debt. The United States has forgiven debt of several foreign nations; now it is time that we forgive the debt of citizens who are descendants of those who helped create the wealth America enjoys today. A history of exploitative policies has denied Blacks the opportunity to build wealth of their own, while using Blacks to build and sustain the wealth and power of white America, with the help and permission of the US government. Action 66 will eliminate this form of bondage once and for all by eliminating all Black debt held or backed by the government.

Action 67

Suspend Income Tax for One Hundred Years

African Americans were brought to this land as commodities, taxed imported goods. Their bodies were taxed, the produce they labored to create was taxed. Meanwhile, they received no benefits of the taxes they generated. After slavery, they paid taxes to a country, states, and cities that denied them services.

Blacks received no protection from law enforcement, only interrogation and brutalization. The district attorney would not investigate crimes in which Blacks were the victims and a white person was the perpetrator. When the houses of Blacks burned down, especially in acts of racial terror, there was no fire department to put it out. Although Blacks paid property taxes, they were sent to poorly funded, segregated, all-Black schools. Black neighborhoods were the last to receive sewer lines and paved streets.

For all these reasons and more, action 67 calls for an abatement for Blacks from property, income, and sales taxes for one hundred years. The purpose of this action is to correct the centuries of taxation without representation or taxation without manifestation of goods and services.

Action 68

Pay Out Insurance Claims to Recover Losses from Massacres

This action calls for payments to insurance policy holders who lost homes, assets, and other real property as a result of white-on-Black race massacres. In Tulsa, for example, the property damage totaled $1.8 million in 1921 dollars, equivalent to $27 million today.[75] Tulsa is only one of many places where no insurance claim was paid for such terrorism.

At the time, insurance companies utilized the "riot clause" in those policies, which prohibited the Blacks from recouping any money from their insurance company even though their premiums had been paid. Meanwhile these insurance companies knew that there was no riot in which Blacks burned down their own houses, nor was it a fair fight between two equal sides that the Blacks provoked. No, in every circumstance of the race massacres in America, the damage was the fault of angry white mobs who were never charged nor held responsible for repairing what they did. In fact, they referred to it as a riot while the Blacks who suffered in it referred to it as a massacre, a disaster, even an attempted genocide.

Action 68 calls on Congress to mandate payment of the claims of all those Blacks who suffered loss during the massacres. The National Association of Insurance Commissioners, which helps to regulate insurance companies, and the Federal Insurance Office, which monitors them, should also step in and withhold licensing from any company that does not pay claims from policy holders who were victimized in a race massacre.

The purpose of this action is to ensure that insurance companies do not get away with denying claims while hiding behind a racist system. In many cases, people rebuilt even though they did not receive the insurance benefits they were due. The money used could have been left as an inheritance for their nearest kin.

Action 69

Open Criminal Investigations into Lynchings, Massacres, and Political Assassinations

The National Association for the Advancement of Colored People states that between the years of 1882 and 1968, "Black people were the primary victims of lynching: 3,446, or about 72 percent of the people lynched, were Black."[76] The Equal Justice Initiative uses a different time frame; from 1877 to 1950, it counts 4,084 racial terror lynchings in twelve southern states and more than three hundred in other states. These acts of racial terror included more than twenty race massacres in places such as Colfax, Louisiana; Wilmington, North Carolina; Atlanta; Tulsa, Oklahoma; and Rosewood, Florida.[77]

Several hundred political leaders who fought for the rights of Blacks were killed. We know about the assassinations of the Rev. Dr. Martin Luther King Jr., Medgar Evers, and Malcolm X, but how about the murders of the Rev. George Wesley Lee, Lamar Smith, Dr. Thomas Brewer, Herbert Lee, and Sammy Younge Jr.? Younge was a Tuskegee native and Navy veteran who was a leader in the Student Nonviolent Coordinating Committee (SNCC). Younge was protesting predominantly white churches and businesses who did not allow Blacks to enter when he was shot in the face and killed.

These violent acts of racial terror greatly destabilized the Black community and the struggle for equality altogether, while the perpetrators of these crimes have rarely been brought to justice. This action calls on the Department of Justice and attorney general to fully investigate all of the acts of racial terror that occurred in this country, from the lynchings to the massacres and assassinations of Blacks and those who sought to fight beside and for them in seeking their liberation. Investigation with the goal of charging and arresting all of those responsible will incredibly aid in increasing the trust which heretofore did not exist between the Blacks and the criminal justice system. In recent years, we have seen unarmed Black people killed by the police for minor infractions, such as traffic violations, while armed white perpetrators who shoot up schools and churches can get arrested without incident. Fully investigating and charging the perpetrators who allegedly murdered Blacks in both past and present would magnificently help repair this gap in trust.

Lastly, the CIA and Department of Justice should report any work they did against civil rights organizations and its leaders. The intelligence agencies can also help investigate who was behind the killing of Black leaders and white leaders like the Kennedys who were helpful to Blacks.

The attorney general's office should partner with organizations like the Innocence Project and Equal Justice Initiative to review cases where racism had been at work in the arrest, jury selection, and sentencing and to provide legal opinions on matters where court cases have not addressed the issue of a crime of racial hatred against Black people.

Action 70

Establish a Racial Terror Compensation Fund

The Foreign Sovereign Immunities Act "authorized U.S. courts to order state sponsors of terrorism—namely, Iran, North Korea, Cuba, and Syria, and previously Libya, Iraq, and Sudan—to pay monetary damages to terrorism victims."[78] Those damages are gathered into a fund for distribution to victims. It is only fair that the United States pay damages to compensate victims of terrorism it has inflicted.

This concept is similar to compensation programs set up for medical and environmental harm to US citizens, including the National Childhood Vaccine Injury Act of 1986, the 1990 Radiation Exposure Compensation Act, and the James Zadroga 9/11 Health and Compensation Act of 2010.

Most programs of this sort start with payment for lost wages. "One researcher took 1860's prices for slaves as an estimate of their labor value and applied compound interest. The result: $2 trillion to $4 trillion."[79] That is money lost from our community that we have never seen. The money that was not paid to the enslaved people remained with slave owners and created more wealth for them to pass down to their children and to invest in other enterprises, while even in freedom Black wealth accrual was systematically limited.

Action 70 calls for the establishment of a compensation fund into which the United States gathers funds to pay damages for state-sponsored slavery, Jim Crow, and racial terror. The victims and descendants of this US-sanctioned and business-supported terrorism will receive compensation commensurate to the time they or their family have been in this country. Payment should be made monthly, tax free, and for a set period of time.

A commission should be established to help oversee the fund, victim eligibility, societal culpability payments, and disbursements. The commission should pursue charges against businesses and organizations that participated in, profited from, or conspired in the exploitation and oppression of Blacks. The fund should be able to grow while formation of the commission and compensation rubrics are set.

Monetary payment of this sort will be necessary to finally and financially make Blacks whole from the dreadful actions of slavery, Jim Crow, racial terror, and all the state-sponsored and sanctioned abuse of Blacks since they arrived in this country.

Action 71

Prioritize Domestic Terrorism and the White Supremacist Threat

Created in 2002 in the aftermath of the September 11, 2001, attack, the Department of Homeland Security is charged with guarding the nation against terrorist threats.

Since 9/11, we have not had another similar attack on American soil. We have, however, had countless mass shootings, acts of terrorism against Asian Americans, and numerous hate crimes against Blacks. In the aftermath of the deadly shooting at an Asian establishment in Atlanta in 2021 and an increase in hate crimes against Asian Americans during the COVID pandemic, a hate crimes bill emphasizing anti-Asian crimes was passed. Nearly ten years after the

Charleston Nine were martyred at Mother Emanuel AME Church, however, no plan has been put in place to protect predominantly Black houses of worship, schools, colleges, or social events. The Black church has been attacked more than any other type of church in America. In 2022 alone, there were a record number of attacks on Historically Black Colleges and Universities (HBCUs)—including a string of bomb threats made by a minor. Historically Black institutions and businesses have been attacked by domestic terrorists with largely no legal ramifications for the perpetrators. In fact, America seems to not even be willing to classify white racial terror as terrorism.[80]

We already know that the biggest domestic threat to the United States of America is white racist extremism. Therefore, the Department of Homeland Security and Federal Bureau of Investigation should utilize their resources to root out and dismantle white supremist organizations and provide annual security updates to Black institutions and leaders on the threats they have uncovered and how they can better safeguard themselves.

Any gathering of more than two hundred Black people should be given the option of having law enforcement protection nearby at no cost to the organization. Protection should also be offered to Black leaders of human rights movements. And historical Black sites (those on the National Register of Historic Places) should receive 24/7 surveillance. Also, when the department is aware of credible threats against Black people or organizations, those targeted should be informed. These actions will help protect the homeland and increase trust between the Black community and those charged with protecting it.

Action 72

Fund Leadership Training Organizations to Restore Black Power Structures

Because of the frightening effect of racial terrorism and the assassination or removal of transformational and generational Black leadership, there has been a vacuum of leadership in Black communities. This action calls for money for historically Black leadership and faith organizations, especially those that were formed during slavery, Jim Crow segregation, or times of racial terror. They include historically Black denominations, such as the African Methodist Episcopal, African Methodist Episcopal Zion, Christian Methodist Episcopal, Missionary Baptist, National Baptist, Primitive Baptist, Progressive Baptist, Church of God in Christ, and Full Gospel Pentecostal churches; sororities and fraternities, such as Kappa Alpha Psi, Alpha Phi Alpha, Omega Psi Phi, Phi Beta Sigma, Iota Phi Theta, Alpha Kappa Alpha, Delta Sigma Theta, Zeta Phi Beta, and Sigma Gamma Rho; and community organizations, such as the Prince Hall Freemasonry and Order of the Eastern Star, Improved Benevolent and Protective Order of the Elks of the World, National Association for the Advancement of Colored People, Black Panther Party, Universal Negro Improvement Association, National Urban League, Southern Christian Leadership Conference, Rainbow PUSH Coalition, Institute of the Black World, and National Action Network.

The purpose of this action is to replenish some of the resources Black organizations have spent to train Americans who have been left out, exploited, or murdered because they sought to uplift and provide services to Blacks who were excluded or oppressed by the United States.

Action 73

Provide Mental Health Care

Mental health care for Blacks should be free and universal, covering at least two visits a year. Dr. Joy DeGruy described in her 2005 book *Post Traumatic Slave Syndrome* how the psychological effects of slavery, racial terrorism, and white supremacist practices have wreaked havoc on Black mental health. Everything from how we raise our children to how we see ourselves and work in everyday environments can be traced back to how our ancestors were treated in this country.

We often limit ourselves, mistrust one another, and don't provide the full support our families and children need because of the mental and psychological warfare that has been inflicted on Blacks in this country. The physical shackles of slavery are gone, but the mental shackles have not been released. Sadly, they are perpetuated and passed down to each successive generation.

As a result, this action calls for free mental health care for Blacks in this nation. Trauma-informed care specifically designed for Blacks and preferably offered by Black mental health providers can provide the psychological support we need to cope and conquer our post-traumatic stress syndromes that originated with and have been perpetuated by white supremacist actions.

Action 74

Provide Medical Health Care

While African Americans were exploited to improve the health of white people (see action 28), their own health continues to suffer. When you look at the rate of diabetes, hypertension, asthma, obesity, and heart disease within the Black community—all higher than in other races—it is no surprise that average life expectancy among Black Americans is a full four years less than for whites.[81] This damage began with changing diets from an African cuisine to a pauper diet in the United States as enslaved people, then was compounded by the stress and trauma endured by our ancestors.[82] The ongoing impact of low-income neighborhoods, food deserts, and minority stress exacerbates the problem.

The health disparity between Blacks and whites is compounded by a widespread mistrust of the majority-white-run health-care system, based on past mistreatment and ongoing racism. The COVID-19 pandemic revealed how severe the consequences of this history are for the modern health of Blacks, with many Blacks refusing to get the COVID vaccine.

Even prior to COVID, however, non-Hispanic white patients utilized a disproportionate amount of the $2.4 trillion spent in 2016 on medical and dental care, nursing facilities, and prescription drugs: they accounted for 72 percent of spending, while comprising only 61 percent of the population, according to a study published in the *Journal of the American Medical Association*.[83] African Americans, who made up 12 percent of the population and accounted for a proportionate 11 percent of the health-care spending, nonetheless "do not receive care until they are experiencing advanced illness," the study found.

> African Americans accounted for 26 percent less spending on outpatient care but 12 percent more spending on emergency department care per person than average, a finding that "reinforces previous research showing unequal access to primary care," the study authors observed.
>
> In contrast, non-Hispanic white Americans received 15 percent more spending per person on outpatient care than average, suggesting they have better access to routine and preventive care.

"This study provides a clear picture of who is benefiting from and who is being left behind in our health care system," said Joseph L. Dieleman, lead author of the study.[84]

It is no surprise Blacks are more likely to lack health insurance than whites.[85] One reason is that the majority of Blacks today still live in the South (56 percent, according to Pew[86]), where most of the states have rejected Medicaid expansion that would insure millions of Americans. This rejection of Medicaid expansion is costing lives and driving up the costs for citizens who lack health insurance and have to resort to the emergency room for care.

Blacks have been denied access to preventative medical care and made objects of medical experimentation for which they have not given consent, been compensated, or received benefit. Repairing such gross medical malpractice can most effectively be done by the government establishing a Repair Care for all Blacks, with benefits similar to those for members of Congress. It is past time that African Americans start to benefit from the great advances they have given to the study of medicine.

Action 75

Recruit and Support Black Medical Professionals

Intertwined with the disparity in access to and use of medical care for African Americans is an understandable mistrust in the medical system—a problem that could be addressed by increasing the number of Black doctors and other health-care providers.

From the genesis of the slave trade and even in the Jim Crow era, many whites believed that Blacks were scientifically inferior to whites and better suited for physical labor than intellectual pursuits. These ideas were buttressed by American physicians like Samuel George Morton and his 1839 book *Crania Americana,* using craniometry, or the size of the cranium, to show that whites were more intelligent than non-whites. His theories were debunked in the book *Mismeasure of Man* by Stephen Jay Gould, published in 1981, a year before I was born; however, the damage caused by Morton went unchecked for well over a hundred years in the medical community, with many scientists seeking to defend Morton's original premise.

Morton's false premise that whites are intellectually superior made it easier for the scientific community to further objectify Blacks, as in the medical experiments previously mentioned and even during the 1920s eugenics movement, when states passed laws (with the support of President Woodrow Wilson) to sterilize the feeble-minded and criminals, with Blacks a primary target.

History tells us a different story of Black intellect and achievement, as Black doctors have been responsible for many medical advancements: Dr. Charles Drew helped create the method of storing blood plasma into blood banks for later transfusion—an innovation that saved countless lives in World War II and in the century since. Dr. Louis Wright administered smallpox vaccine to soldiers with an intradermal method not commonly used, and his daughter Dr. Jane Wright helped show the benefits of combined chemotherapy and the use of methotrexate to treat cancer tumors. Dr. Patricia Bath invented the "Laserphaco Probe" tool for laser cataract surgery. Dr. William Hinton invented the Hinton test to check for syphilis, and Dr. Marilyn Gaston created a penicillin treatment for babies to prevent sickle cell infections later in life.[87] More recently, Dr. Hadiyah-Nicole Green developed a method of treating cancer using lasers and nanoparticles.[88]

Recruiting more talented Black students to the medical field would help remedy the mistrust of medical providers and improve health outcomes for the Black community at large. As one study of Black mistrust in medical researchers states, "A lack of cultural diversity and competence among physicians is a major contributor to African American mistrust of physicians."[89]

To increase the number of Blacks in the medical field, Black students in medical or nursing schools should be able to attend tuition free, allowing them to pursue their education and certification without incurring debt. Those who have graduated already should be able to claim their tuition on their taxes as a deduction.

Action 76

Provide Free Wi-Fi

The internet is one of the most indispensable parts of our life, and our reliance on it for essential functions such as doing work, banking, applying for jobs, managing utilities, making appointments, and doing schoolwork is only increasing. As more and more Americans take internet use for granted, its absence will be more and more detrimental for those who do not have access to it. Blacks have the least amount of access to the internet, especially Blacks in the rural South, of whom 38 percent lack home internet access.[90]

Congress passed a $1 trillion Infrastructure Investment and Jobs Act in August 2021. Sixty-five billion dollars of that will go to "improve broadband internet access in rural areas and make broadband more affordable for lower-income households across the U.S." The bill also aims to address the digital divide in America with a $2.75 billion investment for the Digital Equity Act, targeting underserved communities, and requires rules to stop "'digital redlining,' in which internet providers decline to build or offer access to broadband service in areas deemed unlikely to be profitable."[91]

Actions like this will immeasurably help, but as we have seen with most government actions that are not specifically geared toward African Americans, the deficit Black communities experience may not receive adequate attention. Therefore this action doesn't call just for free Wi-Fi for Blacks who have been left out through digital redlining and poor infrastructure investment but also for procedures and consequences for violations by internet companies. The Federal Communications Commission (FCC) needs to clearly delineate what blocking of access and discrimination looks like in the digital world, what actions constitute violations, and what the punishment is for a violation.

Furthermore, several key provisions were left out of the bill that need to be implemented. For instance, mandate that companies applying for these infrastructure funds ensure their upload and download speed are extremely fast. Speed is important for teleconference or video calls; without it, people cannot adequately compete for jobs nor can students be successful in remote learning. Additionally, municipalities, not private companies, should control the broadband networks. Private companies created this digital redlining in the first place, prioritizing profits over people. Municipalities should be responsible for the oversight of the broadband networks, with the premier goal being equity.

Giving free Wi-Fi to Blacks for fifty years for home and mobile use is vital to their being connected in the world of cyberspace so that they can be competitive in the job market, successful in educational endeavors, and informed in their health decisions. This action, once implemented, can greatly propel Blacks to a position where repair can be realized.

Action 77

Address the Causes and Effects of Environmental Racism

"Environmental racism" describes policies and actions that disproportionately and intentionally direct environmental waste and other harmful effects toward communities of color. It was first recognized by the US General Accounting Office in a 1983 report which "found that 75% of communities near harmful landfill sites were predominantly Black." Since then, the problems identified have grown to include poor water quality, lack of sanitation, soil pollution, noise pollution, and high exposure to carbon dioxide emissions and other chemicals, such as lead in the water in Flint, Michigan, arsenic contamination in San Joaquin Valley, California, and toxic petroleum by-products creating Louisiana's "Cancer Alley."[92]

The amount of wealth in an area plays a significant role in the presence of pollutants. Zip codes are a distinct notable predictor in locating environmental concerns. And yet race is an even higher predictor of air pollution from the oil industry than poverty.[93]

A 2018 study by the Environmental Protection Agency (EPA) used emission particles to compare the environmental burden of pollution across different communities in the U.S. The research found that the burden was 35% higher for people living in poverty in general and 28% higher for People of Color. Black people, specifically, had a burden level 54% greater than that of the overall population.[94]

Predominantly Black communities are being environmentally exploited, and our collective health is suffering from it.

To alleviate the environmental abuse Blacks have suffered, this action proposes mitigation measures the government must take, under the supervision of the EPA. To start with something simple, these actions should include establishing recycling options in every city in America in order to minimize the amount of trash that is sent to landfills (located primarily in Black communities) and surveying each landfill to make sure it is operating in as environmentally sound a manner as possible, meeting not only state but also national and international standards as well.

Soil pollution results from toxic contaminants leaking from landfills, industrial waste, and agricultural pesticides. Soil pollutants, in particular a high level of heavy metals in the soil, can damage the brain, lungs, kidney, liver, and other organs. Long-term exposure can lead to "physical, muscular, and neurological degenerative processes that imitate diseases such as multiple sclerosis, Parkinson's disease, Alzheimer's disease and muscular dystrophy," and can cause cancer.[95]

Soil pollution contributes to water pollution too, as toxic metals seep into the groundwater. Global warming is making matters worse because the warmer the earth gets, the lower the level of groundwater becomes, and the lower the level of groundwater, the higher the concentration of these hazardous chemicals.[96] Data from the EPA "confirms there is unequal access to safe drinking water, based most strongly on race."[97] Water pollution can result from oil spillage, chemical contamination, oxygen depletion, groundwater contamination, and surface water pollution. Even small levels of arsenic in drinking water over time can cause diabetes, cancer, skin damage, and hair loss. Uranium consumed in water over long periods of time causes kidney problems. Regretfully, they are both found in high concentrations in drinking water of predominantly Black communities. Lead is also a common contaminant, due to the outdated piping the water runs through, as in Flint, Michigan. The EPA must make sure that the water and gas pipes in all predominantly Black communities are checked every five years for corrosion.

Particulates in the air are judged by diameter for regulatory purposes. Particles "with a diameter of 10 microns or less (PM10) are inhalable into the lungs and can induce adverse health effects. Fine particulate matter is defined as particles that are 2.5 microns or less in diameter (PM2.5)."[98] Then there is diesel particulate matter (DPM) from diesel exhaust, which is a subset of PM2.5. Neither is good for respiratory well-being, but when they are breathed for prolonged periods of time, the consequences can be extremely detrimental. Asthma, premature death, bronchitis, and lung and heart damage are all possibilities from breathing in particulate matter for even as little as twenty-four hours of exposure.[99] Asthma has become a pandemic within the Black community, especially impacting youth in urban areas, where "African Americans are three times more likely to die from asthma as whites."[100]

Noise pollution also disproportionately affects Black communities due to factories, airports, trains, and traffic near minority neighborhoods.[101] The health effects of noise pollution include high blood pressure, hearing loss, and sleep deprivation.

Radioactive pollution results from nuclear explosions, nuclear power plants, and industry or medicine and can be hazardous for a few hours or a few hundred thousand years—longer than any other form of pollution.[102] "Exposure to large amounts of radioactivity can cause nausea, vomiting, hair loss, diarrhea, hemorrhage, destruction of the intestinal lining, central nervous system damage, and death. It also causes DNA damage and raises the risk of cancer, particularly in young children and fetuses."[103]

Blacks have been exposed to high levels of radiation because of where they live and work. A study reported that Blacks working at the Savannah River Site, a nuclear weapons facility near the South Carolina-Georgia border, between 1951 and 1999 were more likely to have detectable doses of radiation when tested than were non-Black workers. Doses measured in Black females, in particular, were much higher than in white female workers. "The persistence of job segregation and excess radiation exposures of black workers shows the need for further action to address disparities in occupational opportunities and hazardous exposures in the U.S. South,"[104] according to the authors of the study.

Seeing the devastating impact environmental abuses have had on Black people, action 77 calls for multiple steps by the EPA to ensure that each state has an environmental justice plan aimed at lowering the adverse effects of all forms of pollution—including soil, water, air, noise, and radioactive—on Black people. Every new commercial development should have to meet the goals of this new environmental justice plan. Chemical and nuclear facilities must be responsible for either protecting the residents in the surrounding area or providing them with a new and safer place to live at no cost. Industries must be monitored and fined for the waste, pesticides, or heavy metals they produce that find their way into the soil and water of Black communities. Whenever possible, the EPA should hire Black-owned companies to do testing and remediation.

The money collected from these fines, as well as money from the EPA budget, should be provided to Blacks in the form of vouchers to purchase water filtration, air purification, and noise cancellation systems for their homes—again, with preference given to Black-owned companies providing these goods and services. In addition, a fund should be set up to compensate Blacks for the harm already suffered from environmental racism, no less than $100,000 for illnesses suffered and $1 million to each immediate family member if the pollution resulted in death. Last, the EPA should produce an annual racial impact study that shows what pollutants Blacks are exposed to, how, by whom, and how they can best safeguard against them.

Action 78

Solicit Reparations from Slaveholding Sovereign Nations within the United States

Action 78 speaks to other sovereign nations within the United States who owned enslaved people and have yet to give repair— the so-called Five Civilized Tribes: Chickasaw, Choctaw, Seminole, Creek, and Cherokee. These tribal nations received a higher status among European colonizers by adopting certain European practices, though they were also eventually moved from their lands as part of the Indian Removal Act of 1830. Slavery was already a part of the culture for the indigenous Americans, normally as a consequence of military conquest, as it was for most slaveholding cultures prior to European colonialism.

Between 1492 and the time Europeans arrived en masse with their enslaved people, "persons of African ancestry were occasionally adopted as members of the tribes or became members through Indian mothers, however this practice became almost nonexistent as the Indian system of slavery began to be associated with persons of African ancestry and chattel slavery as more and more mixed white tribal citizens brought enslaved Africans into the tribal nations."[105] African enslaved people did for the tribes the same thing they did for the United States: create, build, and sustain wealth. "Prior to the outbreak of the Civil War, African chattel slavery had become a main part of economic wealth for some tribal citizens. Because Indian slavers didn't own personal land, their wealth was based on the number of enslaved Africans they owned."[106] Enslaved people were one of the most valuable material assets they could pass down to their children.

After being brutally relocated through the Trail of Tears, some of the tribes sided with the Confederacy after meeting with Special Commissioner Albert Pike,[107] and ultimately 7,860 Confederate soldiers came from Indian Territory.[108] After the Civil War, the tribes kept their enslaved people for over a full year because the Emancipation Proclamation left out enslaved people in states that were not rebelling against the United States. Likewise the Thirteenth Amendment left out enslaved people in Indian Territory by saying that no slavery "shall exist within the United States, or any place subject to their jurisdiction." Such exclusionary language allowed the tribes to enslave Blacks until the summer of 1866.

Native American tribes suffered genocide and have endured numerous injustices over the centuries, and for this, they clearly have their own reparations claims against the US government that should be honored. However, this does not excuse those tribes that held African American enslaved people from also paying their own reparations to the descendants of the enslaved.

Even more importantly, these tribes must recognize the citizenship of their African American descendants. In the treaties the tribes signed in 1866, they agreed that they would "abolish slavery and accept Freedmen and their descendants as full tribal citizens," but as of yet, not all of the tribes have fully complied with granting citizenship rights.[109] Some tribes have acknowledged the descendants of freedmen as members of the tribe, but none have provided them any reparations. While the government has given some reparations to the indigenous Americans (and more should be given), this action calls on those tribes who owned enslaved people to give repair to them as well.

Action 79

Establish a Bureau for Black Labor

Black workers have always suffered extremely unsafe working conditions, faced discrimination from unions and employers, and received no federal protection until 1964, when Title VII of the Civil Rights Act prohibited employment discrimination based on "race, color, religion, sex, or national origin." Even after this act and the creation of the Equal Employment Opportunity Commission (EEOC) in 1965, actual support for Black workers varies as agencies like the EEOC and Job Corps experience wide variations in funding depending on which political party is in control.

The livelihood of Blacks and repairing the harms of systemic exploitation of Blacks in the American labor system should not be dependent on the ebbs and flows of political shenanigans; therefore, the permanent establishment of a Blacks Bureau with sufficient funding to ensure job training and placement for Blacks in every city and region in America is paramount. As with other agencies, the status and progress of this bureau should be reported to the reparatory justice oversight committee.

The Blacks Bureau would study employment trends of Blacks, train them for jobs, and aid them in finding employment. The bureau would provide technical support for navigating the government contract and procurement process and help to enhance or create a digital and physical Black Wall Street. It would protect unions, because union jobs have helped African Americans become part of the middle class. Private companies now are doing all they can to eliminate collective bargaining, denying employees the right to speak up on their job conditions, wages, and so on.

The Department of Labor has an Occupational Safety and Health Administration, Mine Safety and Health Administration, Wage and Hour Division, Veterans' Employment and Training Service, Office of Disability Employment Policy, Bureau of International Labor Affairs, Women's Bureau, and other important departments—but there is no bureau nor division that focuses on Black people, the most exploited labor force in American history. The establishment of a Blacks Bureau would ensure that Black Americans have the conditions to be successful.

Action 80

Support Black Entrepreneurs

When the Department of Commerce was created in 1903, Congressman Charles Cochran said of its purpose, "We hope to develop new fields of profitable trade and foster old ones. We hope to facilitate industrial development and promote commerce at home and abroad. . . . We will look to this Department to give direction to the energetic campaign that has for its object the conquest of the markets of the world by American merchants and manufacturers."[110]

While the department's mission of creating conditions for economic growth has worked mightily for white-owned businesses, making them global giants in enterprise, these efforts have clearly not been applied equally. According to the census bureau, in 2020 there were 5.6 million American-owned businesses whose ownership could be classified by race and ethnicity, and only 3 percent of them were Black majority-owned. Even worse, they earned only 1 percent of gross profits that year.[111]

Black business owners have always been exploited and under attack. During slavery, those who wanted to enter enterprise could work for their own business only when they had finished with the "master's" work. Then they were cheated by whites on costs and payment. Once emancipated, they faced terrorism fueled by white anger and jealousy that destroyed their businesses. All of this happened with little to no protection from the government to which they paid their taxes. In more recent times, we have seen how Blacks are charged high interest rates.

It is incumbent on the government to repair the hurt and harm caused generationally, collectively, and individually to Black-owned businesses. The three areas of support needed, which are ubiquitous for most Black-owned businesses, are capital, connection, and cash flow.

First, the challenge of getting capital: "Black-owned businesses apply for credit at a rate that is 10 percentage points higher than white-owned firms," reported the *Washington Post*, "but their approval rates are 19 percentage points lower."[112] Even when financing is approved, it is often less than the amount requested. "Only 40 percent of minority-owned firms received the full amount sought compared to 68 percent of white-owned firms—even among firms with comparably good credit scores." Profits follow the money put into the business, with more white-owned businesses reporting profits than Black-owned enterprises.[113]

Second, the lack of connection or peer-to-peer interaction: two-thirds of Black-owned businesses have fewer than ten employees and 17 percent had no paid employees, just the owner and possibly the volunteer labor of family and friends.[114] Hence, connection with other Black-owned businesses is not merely nice but necessary, especially when it comes to competing for contracts from major corporations. Additionally, a better network could assist with technical training, talent acquisition, and career development and coaching.

Last, the problem of cash flow: "Black-owned businesses averaged $58,000 in revenue while White-owned businesses averaged over nine times that amount ($546,000)."[115] Quite often, Black business owners have to forgo paying themselves in order to pay bills. Add the surprise expenses of equipment breaking or customers who are behind in their payments, and you see how lack of cash flow is debilitating.

The Justice Department's Antitrust Division needs to fight harder to remove barriers for start-ups. Black entrepreneurs already have enough challenges; they should not have to contend with established businesses starving them out of the market and stifling their growth. In the hair industry, for example, many African American businesswomen have found it difficult to gain any traction due to suppliers who will not sell them products.[116] Antitrust protections can assist Blacks who have been systematically left out of industry by nefarious actions.

The purpose of this action is to mitigate these issues and do for Black small businesses what America did for other industries during tough economic times. In 2008, President George W. Bush pushed and Congress passed a $700 billion bailout plan for businesses deemed "too big to fail." Today the Black community is in a depression, and our community is too important to fail, so we need the government to act and provide 1 percent of what it gave to businesses in 2008. This money could provide government-backed loans and grants to Black-owned businesses to assist with start-up capital, staffing support, emergency cash flow, and networking associations. These loans will not be based on credit score but on actual and potential annual income. These loans will turn into grants once standards for such things as marketing development, hiring and pay, viability, reinvestment, profit savings, and community support have been met. For instance, for these loans to turn to grants, the government can stipulate that they must hire five people from the community at livable wages and sponsor community activity. If money remains a loan, then they will be charged the prime rate and have sufficient time to pay it back. The networking funds will pay a stipend to individuals who serve as mentors and coaches for the Black-owned businesses.

Action 81

Elevate Africa

Action 81 calls on the State Department to aid in the repatriation of descendants of enslaved people who want to return to their ancestors' homeland. Repatriation should follow a genealogical and DNA study that helps Blacks know exactly where they are from in Africa. The repatriation should be free to the descendants, and a seamless pathway for dual citizenship should be offered.

In addition, better trade policies with African nations should be facilitated for the tribes and kingdoms most adversely impacted by the slave trade. Economics professor Nathan Nunn, who has studied the effect of Africa's slave trades on later economic development, concluded that "'the African countries that are the poorest today are the ones from which the most slaves were taken,' he wrote in the *Quarterly Journal of Economics*."[117]

The effects of European colonialism continue to plague the continent of Africa, which loses more than three times the amount of aid it receives, mainly due to "multinational companies deliberately misreporting the value of their imports or exports to reduce tax," says a 2017 report by Honest Accounts. "Along with these illicit financial flows brain drain, debt servicing, and the costs of climate change—caused predominantly by the west but played out on the world's poorest people—all make Africa a net creditor to the world."[118]

The Department of State should take the lead in forming trade policies that ensure African nations are able to own, refine, and profit from their own resources and prevent Western nations from taking the resources and the profits. The United States should be the chief negotiator in writing a statement of reproach for the actions of all the nations, including the United States, that participated in the slave trade and encourage them to give repair. There should be a reparations treaty that enhances trade negotiations with nations that have given or are in the process of giving repair to descendants of their enslaved people or oppressed groups. Likewise, America should take the lead in building better trade relationships with

African nations most impacted by the slave trade and investing in the African continent as a whole. Since 2014 America has been lagging behind China in terms of investment dollars.

The United States and other Western nations' slave trade resulted in massive amounts of wealth being acquired. Today under the leadership of the secretary of state, America and its allies should begin repairing the harm to which they contributed.

Action 82

Establish a Civil Rights Hotline

Because of the historical problem of racism in the United States, there should be a racism hotline to report problems and a website where videos of racist acts can be uploaded in real time. The website and the hotline will be overseen by the Department of Justice. Acts of racism should not be ignored, and red tape should not prevent people from being able to obtain support and advocacy.

We have seen the many videos of police brutality, most of which were first shared on social media. That platform helped those videos to turn the tide of public opinion toward justice for those victims, but they did little to prevent the injury or death. A website by the Department of Justice would increase the likelihood that federal agents can step in and stop racist behavior. It also serves as a deterrent. Federal agents have nationwide jurisdiction; they can move in and stop local police from violating someone's civil rights and arrest cops for killing a civilian. The hotline would also enable Blacks who may be intimidated from calling local law enforcement to call federal agents and the Department of Justice to intervene.

Action 83

Protect Voting Rights

The right to vote is the most sacred right we have and one that has been denied to African Americans for the majority of our presence in the United States. The Voting Rights Act of 1965 was transformative for Blacks, enabling them to have their voices heard in our democracy; however, since the 2013 Supreme Court ruling in *Shelby County (Alabama) v. Holder* repealed the clearance clause of the act that required some jurisdictions to get approval before changing voting procedures, access to voting and voting rights have been eroding at a rapid pace. Voter identification bills have passed throughout the country making it harder for people to vote. After record-setting turnout in the 2020 presidential election, at least nineteen states enacted thirty-three laws in the first nine months of 2021 that make it harder for citizens to vote. The states that passed restrictive laws are places where it was already difficult to vote.[119] The more restrictive laws limit the number of polling places, make it more difficult to vote by mail, limit early voting, and create other obstacles to casting a ballot.

States should have two polling places open for each of the most local electoral districts (typically that is a city council or alderman ward), allow for early voting, and permit online voting with strong security protocols, including possible use of fingerprint and/or Social Security number. Voting should be at least as easy as buying a gun.

Another thing that would help voter turnout and celebrate the world's oldest democracy is making Election Day a federal holiday, which would allow more people the time to vote.

All of these actions help repair the harm states throughout the nation have inflicted on Blacks to keep them from voting and move our country closer to true democracy in which all citizens can use their right to vote.

Chapter 4

Spiritual Reparations

Spiritual reparations are ways in which communities of faith participate in repairing the harm done spiritually to African Americans. Such harm has been perpetrated in the bombing of predominantly Black churches, the whitewashing of church history and representations of biblical figures, and the promulgation of false doctrine, such as that Black people had no souls and that our skin color was a curse from God. Also not to be ignored is the harm that racism has done to white people's spiritual well-being, as they have deified whiteness and misallocated the grace of God from the blood of Jesus Christ to proximity and assimilation to European culture and the whiteness of one's skin. Needless to say, the body of Christ is in grave need of repair.

Defense of Slavery

In his book *The Color of Compromise,* Jemar Tisby documents in frank detail how the church sanctioned, supported, and solidified white supremacy in the young democracy we call the United States of America.[1] The white churches not only gave sanctuary to racists and slave owners but also provided theological cover with incorrect biblical teachings for those seeking to justify their racism. White supremacy and its children found a home in the predominantly white churches of America, and its children—slavery, Jim Crow, and racial terror—grew together within those four walls built by enslaved people, and an institution became predicated on racial, social, and political hierarchy.

One main reason the white church was a key conspirator in America's original sin is that it was led by people who were also practitioners of racism. Founding fathers of American Christian thought and leaders in the Great Awakening revival movement George Whitefield and Jonathan Edwards owned enslaved people.

Georgia became the thirteenth colony in 1732, and its trustees banned slavery so that European settlers would not have to compete with free slave labor. Whitefield, who needed slavery to financially support his new orphanage, lobbied the colonial government to legalize slavery for the economic benefit of the colony. Whitefield petitioned, "Georgia can never be a flourishing province unless negroes are employed as slaves."[2] Slavery was legalized in Georgia in 1751.

Jonathan Edwards, who many esteem as America's greatest theologian, was a slave owner as well. Objecting to the slave trade because he feared it would inhibit evangelism in Africa, he fully supported slavery in the United States. But unlike others who taught that enslaved people had no souls and were subhuman and not really children of God, Edwards was seen as progressive because he believed enslaved people had souls and should be evangelized but not liberated from earthly shackles. The Great Awakening that Edwards led was effective at spreading Christianity and creating new churches, but it focused and framed the work of the kingdom of God simply on individual salvation and not on dismantling unjust, oppressive systems. Therefore, it was fine to save the souls but shackle the bodies of enslaved people.

Such inconsistent and incomplete ministry is what we see today from many churches who can trace their lineage to this period. Blacks and whites could be seen as spiritual equals, but we do not have to be treated physically, politically, or socially the same. The Baptist General Committee of Virginia in 1793 said as much when it dismissed the discussion of slavery as a "civil issue outside of the scope of the church."[3] Similarly, Presbyterian James Henley Thornwell wrote that the church "has no commission to construct society afresh, . . . to rearrange the distribution of its classes, or to change the forms of its political constitutions."[4] This is the same posture predominantly white churches continue to take on issues they do not want to address, saying racial injustice is a state or civil issue and enabling them to ignore America's racism and unjust policies while proclaiming they care about the souls of Black people. Others actively encourage Christians to not be involved in the transformation of political ideals.

Even those who allowed Blacks in the same worship spaces as whites treated Blacks unequally, not allowing Blacks and whites to sit next to each other in worship. Blacks were relegated to the balcony and could not even kneel at the altar together with whites. Even among leading abolitionists, Blacks were seen as less than whites. Abolitionist and evangelist Charles Finney of Oberlin College supported abolition but was against integration. Such a tepid stance came from the view that individual conversion—not institutional change—would precipitate social transformation.

As slavery became more of a contentious issue in the nineteenth century, mainstream white churches began to practice a more overtly proslavery Christianity. It was rooted in a paternalistic approach that saw Blacks as supremely inferior and unable to live equally with whites. These proslavery Christians saw slavery as a benevolent way to civilize and Christianize the "heathen brute" and considered slave owners to be good Christians so as long as they were gentle to good enslaved people and harsh only when necessary. Moreover, because they thought Blacks could never fully understand, nor make full use of, democratic ideals, Christians such as Presbyterian minister Robert Finley formed the American Colonization Society, which aimed to send free Blacks to Africa. "Could they be sent to Africa, a three-fold benefit would arise: We should be cleared of them; we should send to Africa a population partially civilized and christianized for its benefits; our blacks themselves would be put in better condition."[5]

The Bible was misused and abused to support slavery. Proslavery theologians argued that nowhere in the Bible is slavery prohibited. They used biblical passages and erroneous exegesis of biblical stories such as the curse of Ham (technically the "curse of Canaan," Gen. 9:25) to justify their callous, unchristian, inhuman treatment of Blacks. Speaking to a Confederate group in 1862, Methodist preacher Joel W. Tucker said, "Your cause is the cause of God, the cause of Christ, of humanity. It is a conflict of truth with error—of Bible with Northern infidelity—of pure Christianity with Northern fanaticism."[6]

In the years leading up to the Civil War, the predominantly white churches split well before the nation did, largely over the issue of slavery. The Methodist church in 1844 split over whether bishops could own enslaved people, Baptists split in 1845 over whether missionaries could own enslaved people, and in 1861 the Presbyterians divided over whether they should pledge allegiance to the views of the federal government, in this case, slavery. If the church had been unified in opposition to slavery, there likely never would have been a civil war. But when the church gave theological cover for slavery, it paved the way for proponents of slavery who already had the economic incentive and political power to sustain it.

Religion of the Lost Cause

During the postwar Reconstruction period, when the federal government aimed to give freedom and opportunity to the recently freed enslaved people, the white church decided it was finally time to become active in political life, with a mission to ensure that Blacks never rose above the bottom class in American life. During this era the mythology of the "Lost Cause" spread rapidly. It was the excuse Southerners came up with to explain why they lost the Civil War. It rewrote history to say the Confederates "reluctantly roused themselves to the battlefield not because of bloodlust or a nefarious desire to subjugate black people but because outsiders had threatened their way of life and because honor demanded a reaction."[7]

As a result, organizations such as the Daughters of the Confederacy formed to memorialize those "brave Christian men" who fought for the dignity of the South and the Southern way of life. White churches put memorials to the Confederacy on their property and depicted Robert E. Lee in newly commissioned stained-glass windows alongside biblical heroes.

White supremacist Christians perverted the Christian doctrine of redemption. True Christians know that redemption refers to what God does for sinners, saving us from our sins, through the work of God's son Jesus Christ. "Yet," as Tisby explains, "in the hands of white supremacists a social and political version of redemption justified the racial oppression and violence used to retain white power."[8] So the theological term was weaponized, and the "redeemers" resorted to overtly torturous acts of terror to meet their goals. No group did this more violently than the so-called Christian organization known as the Ku Klux Klan. The Klan's mixture of activities with their ideology became known as Klankraft. A former Grand Dragon of Oklahoma explains it as the "sublime reverence for our Lord and Savior . . . the maintenance of the supremacy of that race of men whose blood is not tainted with the colorful pigments of the universe."[9]

The Ku Klux Klan so perverted Christianity that it transformed the cross, an emblem of Christ's suffering and shame, into a symbol of terror and hatred, all the while claiming to respect the cross and love Jesus and the Word of God. The Klan encourages members to read Romans 12 every day, and in their lodges, the Bible is supposed to be open to that text at all times. As for the cross, they see it as an instrument used to "rally the forces of Christianity against the ever increasing hordes of Anti-Christ. . . . We have added the fire to signify that Christ is the light of the world. As light drives away darkness and gloom so a knowledge of the truth dispels ignorance and superstition."[10]

Ironically, Klankraft is all superstition and an abominable perversion of the gospel of Jesus Christ. They have recklessly misaligned the purpose of Jesus from saving souls and bringing the kingdom of God to earth to elevating and preserving white culture and power. Salvation to them is to have white skin and support "pure" American ideals.

Unlike with slavery, no denominational splits occurred over the work of the "Redeemers," the Lost Cause, or the Ku Klux Klan. These racists were emboldened, nice and cozy in both Baptist and mainline white denominations. In 1915 in Stone Mountain, Georgia, a Methodist preacher named William Simmons used Christianity to revive the Ku Klux Klan; "beneath a makeshift altar glowing in the flickering flames of the burning cross, they laid a U.S. flag, a sword and a Holy Bible."[11] Partly inspired by the film *Birth of a Nation*, the revived Klan started a new wave of terror that included both exploitatively racist governmental policies and the violence of lynchings and race massacres.

After the destruction of Black Wall Street in the place I used to serve, Tulsa, Oklahoma, a Methodist bishop made some explicit, incendiary racist remarks supporting those who had just destroyed the Greenwood District, bombing churches and schools and killing children. Instead of providing comfort to the families of over three hundred Blacks who were killed and dumped in mass graves, this Christian bishop provided encouragement to the perpetrators by saying that he was against racial equality and that separation of the races was "divinely ordained."[12]

Quiet Racism in the Modern Church

Today, openly bigoted views are not seen as polite in most parts of white society and the white church, but neither have they been struck down with the same force with which they were so long upheld. In most white churches to this day, these views have not been scrutinized, condemned, nor even acknowledged by some.

Many white church leaders—even in "liberal" mainline traditions—still have the spiritual laryngitis that hinders them from speaking out against racists and horrific acts of racism. They may be more likely to find their voice when speaking out against people protesting, saying there are better, more polite or civil ways to call for change. It was this hypocrisy that led Dr. King to write the letter from the Birmingham jail, expressing frustration with the "white moderate . . . who prefers a negative peace which is the absence of tension to a positive peace which is the presence of justice."[13] White churches didn't align themselves with the movement for civil rights in the 1950s and 1960s but so many aligned themselves into a conservative voting bloc called the Religious Right in the 1970s and 1980s, which sought to be reactionary to the success of the civil rights movement. Even more recently, white Christians have criticized the Black Lives Matter movement, Colin Kaepernick, and others who protest the killing of unarmed Blacks like Trayvon Martin, Michael Brown, George Floyd, and too many others. And let us not forget that many who joined in on the January 6, 2021, insurrection on the nation's capital claim the name of Christ.

Jemar Tisby referred to these white people's Christianity as compromised. If they do not act now on behalf of reparations, I would say their faith is counterfeit.

We have discussed several passages of Scripture in this book featuring acts of repair, from the Good Samaritan restoring a stranger to health and Zacchaeus paying restitution four times over to those he'd exploited, to the Persian empire restoring the Jews' homeland and temple. Finally, in this chapter written specifically to people of faith, consider God's specific plan of reparations for the people enslaved in a foreign land for four hundred years.

God foresaw the injustice that would befall the Hebrew people, and from the time God established a covenant with Abraham and promised him countless descendants, God warned, "Know this for certain, that your offspring shall be aliens in a land that is not theirs and shall be slaves there, and they shall be oppressed for four hundred years, but I will bring judgment on the nation that they serve, and afterward they shall come out with great possessions" (Gen. 15:13–14).

Centuries later, God ordains Moses to lead the Israelites out of slavery in Egypt and twice repeats this promise that the Egyptians will give them valuable possessions as they depart into freedom.[14] Indeed, after the ten plagues have afflicted the Egyptians and Pharaoh relents and frees the Israelites, he does not send them away empty-handed.

> Then [Pharaoh] summoned Moses and Aaron in the night and said, "Rise up, go away from my people, both you and the Israelites! Go, serve the LORD, as you said. Take your flocks and your herds, as you said, and be gone. And ask a blessing for me, too!"
>
> The Egyptians urged the people to hasten their departure from the land, for they said, "We shall all be dead." So the people took their dough before it was leavened, with their kneading bowls wrapped up in their cloaks on their shoulders. The Israelites had acted according to the word of Moses; they had asked the Egyptians for jewelry of silver and gold and for clothing, and the LORD had given the people favor in the sight of the Egyptians, so that they let them have what they asked. And so they plundered the Egyptians. (Exod. 12:31–36)

Pharaoh and his people send Israel off with livestock, silver, gold, and clothing. While the word *plundered* in verse 36 may sound like Israel robbed the Egyptians of these valuables (which the verse says the Egyptians gave freely), it is the same Hebrew word used in Ezekiel 14:14 that is translated "save," "rescue," or "deliver," depending on the translation.[15] Read in that way, the Israelites' acceptance of the Egyptians' payment seems more like the blessing Pharaoh asked for. It suggests that the Egyptians are being redeemed of their sin against the Israelites through the payment of this restitution. According to Old Testament professor Matthew Schlimm, "The Egyptians have already faced an onslaught of plagues, and they dread more coming. . . . The Israelites *rescue* the Egyptians from God's ongoing judgment by asking for and receiving their valuables."[16]

Spiritual repair is needed as much as any other form of repair. The white church in America can use its networks and influence to show that reparations is not simply a political pursuit but a spiritual one as well—one with the power to transform our country for the better. "Reparations benefit not just the oppressed but also the oppressors," writes Schlimm.[17] So listen, white church: the prayers, protests, and petitioning of your brothers and sisters in Christ for the cause of repair could help turn the political tide in America toward this most Christian ideal of redemption.

Action 84

Form a Church Reparations Committee

Predominantly white churches should first establish a reparations committee. Both at the denominational and congregational levels, these bodies are needed to thoughtfully determine ways repair could be given, beginning with research and acknowledgment, as outlined below, and to oversee all of the activities, initiatives, and events that will emerge in pursuit of the goal. Honestly, seeking repair from the faith community is a yeoman's task. The resistance shown by generations of white Christians before you will be directed at this team, and you will need strength in numbers and in Christ to carry out your mission. Therefore, it will be efficacious to collaborate with members and leaders of other congregations and denominations, supporting one another to see how we can let God's will be done on earth as it is in heaven.

As reparations involve not just talk but resources, this committee will seek funds and assist with their distribution. Enslaved people built many houses of worship before 1865, and money made from slave labor supported these churches. Even if your building is newer and your endowment established long after slavery, the wealth that enabled both likely has roots in unfairly gotten gains. As we have seen throughout this book, benefits reaped or denied in one generation have impact on generations to come. Portions of endowments, Sunday offerings, and so on should be set aside for the church's reparations fund. This fund could be used to put on the actions called for in this chapter and even more.

It is past time for us as a church to stop paying lip service to racial unity. There is a need for just donation to Black churches and communities without any strings attached. As we ask our members to give to us as unto the Lord with no earmarks, when we are doing God's work we should give it to those or their descendants whom we know have been wronged.

The purpose of this committee is to make sure that the faith community has the resources it needs to repair from all racial harm in which they have been complicit.

Action 85

Research Your Church's History

The historical details involving slave ownership and transport in the United States are hard to come by. Blacks have spent generations researching, trying to identify their ancestors. The benefits of researching the church's history are twofold: First, knowing how your congregation and its members participated in slavery, racial terrorism, and segregation will help inform why and how your church performs its reparations. Second, the records of white churches can be helpful for Blacks' genealogical research.

The archives of white churches can contain lists of the enslaved people purchased and sold by the church, and they often have the infrastructure, volunteers, and members with connections to help get Black families the information they need to find their ancestors. Archives may also contain newspaper articles on events of major importance to the Black community, such as lynchings, massacres, and civil rights debates. The church can also research the ownership of its land and adjacent sites to be sure that Blacks who may have suffered from land theft have the facts needed to pursue justice.

Reparation is also about information, which was lost and, in some cases, discarded. Blacks were robbed of information about their ancestors because they were treated as chattel and not human. It is incumbent on the white churches to assist as much as they can so that we can all know more about our lineage, land, and the history we share.

Action 86

Fund Black Church Renovations

Historically Black churches' buildings are some of the oldest and most neglected in the communities they serve. Seen as a place of community service and worship, the buildings belong to Black churches that seldom take the needed time or resources to care for them.

Many congregations have suffered some sort of racial violence, insurance claim discrimination, local political pressure to sell, and other factors that have impacted why the buildings are in the shape

they are in. Many Black churches were attacked by white supremacists, others by urban renewal that displaced church membership,
others by the building of highways or housing projects, jails, and
so on near the church. In addition, because Black churches are for
the most part still in the Black community where property value is
low, the equity to do renovations is very low. Black churches have
a great need for long-term financial sustainability.

Hence, this action calls on predominantly white churches to
assist in setting up and funding endowments to support the upkeep
and renovation of Black church buildings and help make these historical and cultural community icons into landmarks.

Action 87

Fund Black Pastor Sabbaticals

Burnout among all clergy is a very real problem. Pastors have a
messiah complex that encourages us to work hard and deny ourselves the simple pleasures of rest. Most churches are understaffed
and rely on more volunteers than paid staff. Senior pastors are the
highest paid and even that is rarely enough for them to not have
to supplement their income. Burnout has driven many out of the
ministry, torn families apart, and even led to suicide. This is especially true among Black clergy.

Black clergy have the normal responsibilities of any other clergyperson (which in the tech age often includes being the web
administrator in addition to being the pastor, counselor, eulogist,
lead worshiper, janitor, receptionist, tour guide, and handyman),
but historically, Black pastors have the added load of being a community leader and voice of the Black community. Their responsibility is to care for a community, not just a congregation.

The normal activity of pastors and the biblical example set by
Jesus are reasons for any pastors to take a sabbatical. The added
pressure Black pastors feel in responding to racial community
trauma, speaking to the needs of Black people, and pastoring
churches that have been neglected, systematically attacked, and
culturally degraded is even more reason why Black pastors should

receive paid sabbatical sponsored by our friends of the faith. A predominantly white church or member within could sponsor a pastor's time away, which would include paying for the pastor's replacement and salary. Even better would be a travel stipend, because many do not get paid enough to go on a long, restful vacation.

Action 88

Organize Church Listening Sessions

We can no longer take for granted that the toil and travail of Black people, churches, and communities are well-known. Living in Tulsa taught me that you can have two different communities residing in the same city with two different histories or stories about the same incident, and the descendants of both victims and perpetrators can be ignorant of all that has occurred. In Tulsa, for decades, Blacks were intimidated into silence. Across America too much Black history has been silenced or erased.

This action calls on Black and white churches to fellowship together for the main purpose of listening. God anatomically gave us two ears and one mouth. I truly believe the great designer and creator of humankind was seeking to show us that we should listen twice as much as we speak. The goal of these sessions is not to be heard but to listen to what is being said. Listen to people who look different from you. White people especially—listen. Blacks have too often been forced to be silent about their suffering and agony. White brothers and sisters in Christ, listen first to the stories of your Black neighbors in fellowship.

Invite a historian or facilitator to manage the session. After listening, take time for reflection, then deliberative dialogue.

Action 89

Engage in Racial Awareness Conference Education

Building on the listening sessions of action 88, predominantly white denominations and churches should have regular education conferences on racism, reparations, and repentance. Invite an experienced Black educator (this author could be made available to assist) and organize your conference around their leadership. Participants should be educated on the plight of Black people, the role white faith institutions played in subjugating and promulgating white supremacy, the impact it had on the country, and ways to repent and atone for those actions. In these conferences, attendees will also learn about how racism is a sin and the true universality of God's creation. Last, the conference should speak to the contributions of Africans to the Bible and church history.

White people have the privilege of rarely thinking about race. The purpose of this action is to educate the participants on how the current socioeconomic status of Blacks started hundreds of years ago and how white supremacy has functioned in the past and continues to operate today. Conferences should encourage the attendees to repent and repair.

Action 90

Study Publications on Religion and Racism

Organize study groups or assign existing Sunday school and Bible study groups to read books or articles on both the historical and contemporary racial context of America and how they intersect with our faith. Consider the publications referenced in this book and others that include empirical data, cultural analysis, the role of the church, and stories of triumph by Blacks.

Spiritual repair should include academic theological research into the erroneous biblical interpretations underpinning racist beliefs. Learn the truth about the Bible and human history. Look for books and articles in which churches have researched and acknowledged the role of their actions and teachings and how they aided and even produced acts of racism. Seek out literature on how the consequences of those actions can be mitigated and eradicated by the church. This book could be a resource as well, of course.

Don't be afraid to read about the ill effects of racism, especially when it is produced from communities of a Christian faith tradition. American Christians tend to focus on how other religions, namely Islam, inspire people who have committed heinous acts of terrorism. We cannot ignore the religious underpinnings of white supremist groups such as the Ku Klux Klan and the origins of their violent racist theology. Members of hate groups active today most likely attend or grew up in predominantly white churches. Saying that people who hold racist beliefs are not "real Christians" is not helpful and keeps us from engaging honestly with our history and theology.

Action 91

Hold Racism Repentance Revivals

Revivals have served a pivotal role in shaping American Christianity. Revivals were used in both the First and Second Great Awakenings. Famous events include the Cane Ridge Revival and Azusa Street Revival, but countless churches host annual revivals each year. Revivals are worship services with the explicit purpose of reinvigorating Christians who have grown spiritually arid. Typically they last for days, if not weeks, and are normally preceded by prayer meetings to spiritually set the atmosphere and petition God for the objective of the revival to be met.

The American church needs a revival. Sure, we have them all of the time—well, some of us still do. However, seeing as the sin of racism and the idolatry of white supremacy have shackled the predominantly white churches for far too long, racism repentance revivals have the potential of saving countless souls and breaking the oldest yoke on the American church: racism. We need a seven-year-long continuous revival of multiple denominations throughout the country, or even the world. The pervasiveness of white supremacy has infected virtually every place where European white Christians have gone.

Why seven years? God made the world in six days, rested on the seventh, and made it holy. Joshua walked around the wall of Jericho for seven days, and on the seventh day seven times. Seven represents completion. Just as the seventh day is holy, the seventh year will be a magnanimous time of completion and praise, seeing what God has done in and through those attending. These revivals over the course of seven years could change not just the church but the nation and world. Biblically, seven sets of seven years precede a year of jubilee. In fifty years, even greater work unifying the kingdom of God will occur. That, however, will have to be led and organized by the next generation. I pray to be alive to see it.

Action 92

Redirect Foreign Missions to a Black Church

Global mission work is something on which predominantly white churches spend an exorbitant amount. Hundreds of billions of dollars each year are spent on foreign missions, a fraction of which could be set aside for inner-city investment in the Black community and predominantly Black churches. It is the height of spiritual hypocrisy for predominantly white churches to focus all their mission budgets on overseas work when the bitter fruit of their sinful racist habits have produced a harvest here at home that has plagued and sickened those who have digested it. First repair the harm you have caused in America before you go and ride in on your high horse to other noble civilizations, infecting them with your brand of Western, whitewashed, Eurocentric, neoconservative, soul-solely, apolitical, ahistoric, greed- and prosperity-based form of Christianity.

This action calls on US church missions to adopt a Black church—not to give them spiritual leadership, to be clear—to assist with church expenses and volunteer power. While I was pastoring in Tulsa, Boston Avenue United Methodist Church sent volunteers daily to aid Vernon AME Church in our food ministry and supported it financially, as did All Souls Unitarian Church and some white friends and allies who attended other churches. Vernon was blessed with several philanthropic nonprofits who supported us, but the work of churches and individuals led by their faith meant so much because they were exemplifying the spirit of unity that Christ calls for.

This simple reallocation of some funds from foreign to domestic missions can make a huge difference for Black and white churches alike. White churches' theology, policy, and practice have caused many Black churches and the communities they represent to be in great need. From personal experience, I can say that the volunteers and churches who participate will receive much more benefit from it than those they are led to serve.

Action 93

Teach Whole History in Church School and Seminaries

Church school is the bedrock for Christian education. Local churches essentially have what is akin to a conference each week. Lesson plans are created by pastors or writers at the denominational level. But where do those pastors and writers learn about America's racial history?

Seminaries train future clergy and lay leaders. Unfortunately, the whole history of what happened in the United States is not taught, and the whole history of what America did to its own citizens is not shared either.

Every seminary of the predominantly white churches should have an African American history department and courses that speak to the dangers of religious racism that has been practiced in America and how it can be discarded. Early church history should emphasize that some of the oldest churches in the world are in Africa. Biblical studies courses should be specific in dismantling the erroneous doctrines like the "curse of Ham." The pseudoscience that taught Black inferiority and segregation-supporting tenets were taught in the church and seminaries, so anti-racist theology and the fact that the church could do such things should be taught as well. Predominantly white churches should learn from the faith of Black churches in teaching how resilience, faith, and fortitude were exemplified. The importance of repentance, reparation, and reconciliation should be taught with as much emphasis as the recognition of sin. Then a true revival can take place.

Action 94

Confess, Apologize, and Denounce Racism as a Church

As your congregation or denomination undertakes these practices to understand the harms of racism, there will come a time for a confession of how the church aided and abetted racism and white supremacy. Acknowledge the harm done as specifically and publicly as possible.

Confession should be followed by an apology. Contrition should be felt and repentance practiced and institutionalized. Formally denounce racism in all its forms, especially as it has been perpetuated by the church and blasphemously in the name of God.

Most church mission statements summarize what the church stands for, a set of values that describe the mission of the organization. A way of making repair as a church is to publicly denounce racism in your mission statement. The following example can be modified for use in your context: "We denounce racism and all manifestations of white supremacy. This organization seeks to eliminate the by-products of racism and repair the injustice that has been done. As a community of believers we know nothing is too hard for God."

Action 95

Rename Church Properties Named for Unrepentant Slaveholders

Slavery was a grossly horrific event in American history, but it brought in hundreds of millions of dollars. Many of those profiteers gave generously to their churches, resulting in seminary buildings, fellowship halls, even sanctuaries built with the money of oppression.

As a sign of indebtedness to their benefactors, some of these congregations named these holy places after them. As with streets, schools, and public buildings named after slave owners and segregationists (see action 15), retaining these names sends a message that their actions are still condoned and supported by the community—and how much worse that message is coming from a Christian congregation. As a sign of regeneration from a racist past, churches should change their names if they are found to have had a brutally racist past.

In the Bible, name changes happen when a person receives a new insight, sense of purpose, or redirection. The names of Abram and Sarai are changed to Abraham and Sarah in Genesis 17. Jacob's name is changed to Israel after he wrestles with the angel in Genesis 32. Jesus changes Simon's name to Peter in Matthew 16:16–18. Name changes are spiritually significant because they denote growth. In Abraham's case, it showed God's promise, with Jacob it showed how he overcame his past, and with Peter it showed his faith. For churches with property named after slave owners and racists, a name change can symbolize their overcoming a sinful past, stepping out in faith, and walking into the promise God has for them.

Action 96

Decolonize Your Hymnal

Music is an integral part of worship. It almost is synonymous with worship. Music moves the soul and excites the heart. Lyrics of songs sung during worship motivate us to praise and prepare our hearts to worship.

Does your hymnal reflect only European American traditions? If so, you need to decolonize your hymnal just as you decolonized your bookshelf in action 4. This action calls on predominantly white churches to expand their hymnals to include songs written and composed by Blacks. Include genres such as Negro spirituals and the Black national anthem, "Lift Every Voice and Sing." Church hymnals should be as diverse as the body of Christ. When we get to heaven, we will be joined by people from every nation and tongue, and our hymnals should reflect that. Especially in America with its history of racism, there should be an affirmative effort to include Black voices in the book of songs. These songs provide a glimpse of the trials, travails, and faith of members of the body of Christ who have endured much.

Incorporating these songs into worship will give your

congregation a greater appreciation for Black spiritual music, which is a form of repair as it gives white Christians another lens through which Black suffering and triumph can be seen. Because no royalties were ever paid for Negro spirituals, this action also calls for churches to designate a Black gospel music fund to help Black churches buy instruments, pay musicians, and put on gospel concerts. This repair can enhance the arts of the Black church, which has given birth to many forms of music in America, from country to rock and roll and R & B.

Action 97

Contract with Black Businesses

Churches are an economic ecosystem all by themselves. Predominantly white churches were funded by offerings from people who benefited from slavery and an oppressive economic system that exploited Blacks.

Many Black-owned businesses have been left behind by a racist system that has discriminated against them and manipulated prices (grossly underbidding Black businesses to run them out). Because they generationally have been denied wealth-building opportunities, Black-owned businesses cannot readily lower their prices as much as white-owned businesses either. Churches have both discretion on how to use funds and the stated goal of helping those in need. Churches do not have to go through a public process, so there is no public oversight nor is there a mandate to accept the lowest bid. In the past, these private decisions allowed for them to choose all white vendors, leaving Black vendors out of the mix.

Hence, this action calls on churches to help repair Black businesses by hiring at least one Black-owned business for contractual services. If churches already have one, they should seek to use two. Economic justice is a major plank in reparations. Churches can help lead and provide an example for the nation. These are services that churches already utilize, so it should not add much to the overall budget, but it directs money where the need is the greatest, which matches perfectly with the mission of these churches.

Action 98

Establish a Denominational Black Caucus

Predominantly white churches in recent decades have increased their number of Black ministers and leaders. Such a development is extremely positive for diversity and kingdom growth. Nonetheless the people in these positions are only as effective as the support they receive. Professional development, peer networking, conferences, mentoring, and job coaching are the type of support that Black ministers and leaders should receive from these predominantly white denominations.

The positions given to Blacks are a positive sign, but positions with no power nor peer networking or comprehensive professional development produce a false sense of inclusion with no equity. During slavery, white churches had Black preachers, but they had no autonomy nor agency and, of course, little to no pay. To repair this egregious wrong, predominantly white churches should provide these supports and enhancements to their system and offer cultural training for the general administration staff to better work with their Black staff members. The National Black Presbyterian Caucus in the Presbyterian Church (U.S.A.) and Black Methodists for Church Renewal (a caucus in the United Methodist Church) model the kind of networking and support Black clergy need.

If your denomination or network of congregations does not already have such a group, work to establish one in order to help repair the harm of the maltreatment of Black staff, clergy, and administration and to provide a road map for not just inclusion but equity at the workplace.

Action 99

Celebrate Black History Month and Juneteenth

Black history is American history, but unfortunately it is not treated as such. The vast, voluminous history of Black people in America cannot fully be captured in a month. However, churches should honor February as Black History Month and seek to highlight the annals of Black American history. Sing hymns and gospel songs from the Black tradition, study historic speeches and letters in Sunday school, and participate in community festivities with your Black neighbors. Celebrating Juneteenth (which as of 2021 is a national holiday in the United States) is another way to honor the history of Black Americans as a congregation.

In planning these programs and activities, churches should rely on people who are knowledgeable and have great passion for sharing Black history in a meaningful way. If needed, a consultant should be brought in to work with the program committee to ensure the programming is respectful, truthful, and meaningful to the participants, audience, church, and community.

These celebrations can help repair the harm and abominable neglect of Black contributions to American society. Such acknowledgment is even more urgent when you consider how the teaching of Black history (erroneously labeled "critical race theory") is now being banned in several states. With the growing number of Blacks in predominantly white churches, this effort of repair could also help Black parishioners to feel more welcome and appreciated.

Action 100

Destroy the Idol of a White Jesus

One of the worst actions taken by predominantly white churches over the centuries is making a graven image of God and putting white skin on the creator of the universe. Everywhere you look— from the Vatican to Vermont—God, Jesus, angelic beings, and biblical characters all appear to be white. Never mind there is absolutely no text in the Bible that says any of them are white. Historically, human characters in the Bible would have been Middle Eastern, with brown skin. Meanwhile, there are several texts in which Jesus is described having feet like bronze, eyes like fire, and hair like wool. Very Afrocentric descriptions: bronze is very dark brown, eyes like fire would be brown eyes, and hair like wool describes coarse, very curly hair.

Sadly, the white church has so whitewashed the history of

Christianity that people see it as a "white man's" religion. The imagery used and promulgated has caused Blacks and other non-whites to exercise extreme faith in a god who has been presented to them only in the image of their oppressors. Tragically, many have been unable to look beyond this abhorrent ahistorical and nonbiblical depiction of Jesus and have chosen not to be a part of the Christian religion. White supremacy has stained the gospel and caused many to never turn to Christ. While that is a decision those people will have to answer for, those who present whiteness as normative and have buttressed the theology and idolatry of white supremacy will have to answer for their actions as well.

One of the Ten Commandments prohibits the creation of "graven images," which Jews and Muslims take very seriously, avoiding any artistic representation of divine beings. White people, however, created an image of God that looked like them and gave some divine quality to their skin. This single solitary action became the central basis of white supremacy, and it was promulgated through the church, ruining people's innocent, pure view of God and imposing a Western white portrayal of not just God but all the biblical and heavenly characters. Today what we unfortunately have is worship not of the God of the Bible but of the god or idol of white supremacy. It is here where the church and whiteness go hand in hand and any threat to white culture becomes a threat to Christian values.

To follow the Ten Commandments, cease making images of the face or likeness of God. When creating art or choosing illustrated resources like children's Bibles and curricula, we must take care to choose more historically accurate images of Jesus Christ and all humans described in Scripture. We must repent of our idolatry that has worshiped whiteness and called it divine.

Benediction

*A*nyone who has harmed Black America should aid in repairing Black America. Reparations is the most morally righteous action America needs to take, correcting its first and worst sin. In this book, you have seen an array of recommendations that could help make the whole of America truly whole. From institutional land grants, repatriation, direct payments, and debt forgiveness, to criminal justice reform and other forms of repair, to societal and individual acts of support, and spiritual acts of atonement, these actions are needed to close the humongous gap between right and wrong within halls of faith and throughout the country. This is my act of hope for America, presenting actions to repair injustices and create equity so that this greatest country on earth can soar to higher heights.

We are a nation born out of a revolution. It is now time for revolutionaries to arise again, armed not with muskets and bayonets but with mission and backbone to fight against the imperialism of ignorance and hordes of hate. It is time to lift up and inscribe a new declaration of independence, not from Great Britain but from great greed, great racism, and great white supremacy. Let us all fight the good fight, in God we trust. In this ethos, I pray that God may bless America in the name of the greatest act of repair himself, Jesus Christ, my Lord and Savior. Amen!

Questions for Reflection
and Discussion

Chapter 1: Individual Reparations

1. Do you know your family's history in relation to slavery? How would you describe your relationship to America's racist past?
2. If it is true that "it is not purely the malice of individuals that prevents equality, but the laws, structures, and norms of a society" (p. 15), what do you see as the role of individuals in creating a more equal society?
3. What new information have you learned about African American history? What do you want to learn more about?
4. What three actions of individual reparations can you commit to doing?
5. What are some challenges you may face while taking these actions? What are some areas in which you need to grow in order to overcome these challenges?
6. What other forms of individual reparations can you think of?

Chapter 2: Societal Reparations

1. In what ways do you see society still treating whiteness as a "public and psychological wage," to use W. E. B. DuBois' term (p. 41)?
2. Without laws forcing action to be taken, how do you think neighborhoods, cities, civic organizations, and businesses can best be motivated to take reparative actions like those listed in chapter 2?

3. Does your neighborhood have a racially restrictive covenant? Can you think of local streets, schools, or monuments honoring slaveholders or Confederate leaders? Are you in a line of work that historically or currently causes harm or limits opportunity for African Americans?

4. What three actions of societal reparations can you commit to advocate for with the appropriate groups?

5. From whom do you expect to encounter resistance while taking these actions? How can you prepare to stand up to or work through this resistance?

6. What other forms of societal reparations can you think of?

Chapter 3: Institutional Reparations

1. Have you or your ancestors benefited from government policies like a government-backed, low-interest home loan, Social Security, or the GI Bill? How would your family's life be different if those benefits had not been available to you?

2. Are there certain areas of institutional racism you feel especially moved to explore further or take action on (for example, criminal justice, education, or commerce)?

3. What three actions of institutional reparations can you commit to advocate for with your neighbors and elected officials? How will you do that?

4. How will you respond to those who say it would be too expensive to implement a national program of government reparations?

5. How do you think the United States would be different after reparations are made to Black Americans?

6. What other forms of institutional reparations can you think of?

Chapter 4: Spiritual Reparations

1. Does your church talk about racial justice? If not, what needs to happen for the congregation to be willing to take action for spiritual reparations?

2. How does your (or your church's) theology promote or hinder racial equality and justice? Consider things like the way you picture Jesus, your definition of sin, and the way you believe God wants Christians to engage with problems in the world.

3. What is your church's history in relation to slavery, segregation, and interracial ministry?

4. What three actions of spiritual reparations can you commit to discussing with your pastor or congregational leaders?

5. From whom do you expect to encounter resistance while taking these actions? How will you respond? What will you do if your congregation refuses to take action?

6. Consider Matthew Schlimm's statement (p. 150), "Reparations benefit not just the oppressed but also the oppressors." How do you think the United States will be different—for people of all races—after reparations are made to Black Americans?

Notes

Foreword

1. National Public Radio, "Read Martin Luther King Jr.'s 'I Have a Dream' Speech in Its Entirety," *Talk of the Nation,* updated January 16, 2023, https://www.npr.org/2010/01/18/122701268/i-have-a-dream-speech-in-its-entirety.

2. National Public Radio.

Introduction

1. UN General Assembly, Resolution 60/147, Basic Principles and Guidelines on the Right to a Remedy and Reparation for Victims of Gross Violations of International Human Rights Law and Serious Violations of International Humanitarian Law, A/RES/60/147 (March 21, 2006), https://www.ohchr.org/en/instruments-mechanisms/instruments/basic-principles-and-guidelines-right-remedy-and-reparation.

2. "What Are Reparations?," National Coalition of Blacks for Reparations in America, accessed August 26, 2023, https://ncobraphl.org/why-reparations/what-are-reparations/.

3. "Reparations Now Toolkit," Movement for Black Lives, 2019, download available at https://m4bl.org/policy-platforms/reparations/.

Chapter 1: Individual Reparations

1. Claud Anderson, *Black Labor, White Wealth: The Search for Power and Economic Justice* (Bethesda, MD: PowerNomics, 1994).

2. Jonathan Weisman and Reid J. Epstein, "G.O.P. Declares Jan. 6 Attack 'Legitimate Political Discourse,'" *New York Times,* February 4, 2022, https://www.nytimes.com/2022/02/04/us/politics/republicans-jan-6-cheney-censure.html.

3. "Report to the United Nations on Racial Disparities in the U.S. Criminal Justice System," Sentencing Project, April 19, 2018, https://www.sentencingproject.org/reports/report-to-the-united-nations-on-racial-disparities-in-the-u-s-criminal-justice-system/.

4. Charlton McIlwain, "Of Course Technology Perpetuates Racism. It Was Designed That Way," *MIT Technology Review*, June 3, 2020, https://www.technologyreview.com/2020/06/03/1002589/technology-perpetuates-racism-by-design-simulmatics-charlton-mcilwain/.

5. Equal Justice Initiative, "Lynching in America: Confronting the Legacy of Racial Terror," 3rd ed. (Montgomery, AL: Equal Justice Initiative, 2017), https://eji.org/reports/lynching-in-america/.

6. Randy Krehbiel, "Tulsa Race Massacre: Black Tulsans Were Detained in Camps throughout the City," *Tulsa World,* May 31, 2020, https://tulsaworld.com/tulsa-race-massacre-black-tulsans-were-detained-in-camps-throughout-the-city/article_45c3eb63-29f0-5b25-b4fc-f3968c3426fd.html.

7. Victor Luckerson, "What a Florida Reparations Case Can Teach Us about Justice in America," *Time*, September 10, 2020, https://time.com/5887247/reparations-america-rosewood-massacre/.

8. Wendy Sawyer and Peter Wagner, "Mass Incarceration: The Whole Pie 2020," Prison Policy Initiative, March 24, 2020, https://www.prisonpolicy.org/reports/pie2020.html#slideshows/slideshow1/2.

9. "ACLU Lawsuit Goes after $2 Billion Bail Industry That Profits Off Poor People," American Civil Liberties Union, April 17, 2019, https://www.aclu.org/press-releases/aclu-lawsuit-goes-after-2-billion-bail-industry-profits-poor-people.

10. David Arnold, Will Dobbie, and Crystal S. Yang, "Racial Bias in Bail Decisions," May 2018, https://economics.harvard.edu/files/economics/files/ms27542.pdf.

11. Peggy McIntosh, "White Privilege and Male Privilege: A Personal Account of Coming to See Correspondences through Work in Women's Studies," Wellesley Centers for Women, 1988, download available at https://www.wcwonline.org/Fact-Sheets-Briefs/white-privilege-and-male-privilege-a-personal-account-of-coming-to-see-correspondences-through-work-in-women-s-studies-2.

12. Curtis Bunn, "Report: Black People Are Still Killed by Police at a Higher Rate than Other Groups," *NBC News*, March 3, 2022, https://www.nbcnews.com/news/nbcblk/report-black-people-are-still-killed-police-higher-rate-groups-rcna17169.

13. "The High Price of Bail," Justice Policy Institute, accessed April 12, 2022, https://justicepolicy.org/wp-content/uploads/2022/02/high_price_of_bail_-_final.pdf.

14. Danielle Paquette, "One in Nine Black Children Has Had a Parent in Prison," *Washington Post*, October 27, 2015, https://www.washingtonpost.com/news/wonk/wp/2015/10/27/one-in-nine-black-children-have-had-a-parent-in-prison/.

15. Katrina vanden Heuvel, "The Staggeringly High Price of a Prison Phone Call," *Washington Post,* November 30, 2021, https://www.washingtonpost.com/opinions/2021/11/30/staggeringly-high-price-prison-phone-call/.

Chapter 2: Societal Reparations

1. "Blumenbach and the Concept of Race," Georg-August-Universität Göttingen, Germany, accessed November 7, 2023, https://www.uni-goettingen .de/en/650077.html.

2. W. E. B. DuBois, *Black Reconstruction in America* (1935; repr., New York: Free Press, 1998), 700–701.

3. Ximena Bustillo, "Black Farmers Call for Justice from the USDA," NPR, February 12, 2023, https://www.npr.org/2023/02/12/1151731232/black -farmers-call-for-justice-from-usda.

4. Robin DiAngelo, *White Fragility: Why It's So Hard for White People to Talk about Racism* (Boston: Beacon, 2018).

5. Amanda Holpuch, "Illinois Homeowners Can Now Remove Racist Clauses from Their Property Deeds," *New York Times*, January 20, 2022, https://www.nytimes.com/2022/01/20/us/illinois-housing-deed-racism.html.

6. Southern Poverty Law Center, "Whose Heritage? Public Symbols of the Confederacy," 3rd ed., 2022, https://www.splcenter.org/20220201/whose -heritage-public-symbols-confederacy-third-edition.

7. "List of Confederate Monuments and Memorials in Alabama," Wikipedia, https://en.wikipedia.org/wiki/List_of_Confederate_monuments _and_memorials_in_Alabama.

8. Southern Poverty Law Center, "Whose Heritage? Map," https://www .splcenter.org/whose-heritage-map.

9. Emmanuel Felton, "Alabama Spends More Than a Half-Million Dollars a Year on a Confederate Memorial. Black Historical Sites Struggle to Keep Their Doors Open," *Washington Post*, October 4, 2021, https://www.washingtonpost .com/national/alabama-spends-more-than-a-half-million-dollars-a-year-on -a-confederate-memorial-black-historical-sites-struggle-to-keep-their-doors -open/2021/10/03/77953f7e-222a-11ec-8fd4-57a5d9bf4b47_story.html.

10. Bonnie Berkowitz and Adrian Blanco, "A Record Number of Confederate Monuments Fell in 2020, but Hundreds Still Stand. Here's Where," *Washington Post*, updated March 12, 2021, https://www.washingtonpost.com /graphics/2020/national/confederate-monuments/.

11. Maya Brown, "Proposed Alabama Bills Would Protect Confederate Monuments and Raise Fines If They're Removed," CNN, February 9, 2022, https://www.cnn.com/2022/02/09/us/alabama-confederate-monuments-bills /index.html.

12. *Oxford English Dictionary*, s.v. "cultural appropriation, n.," July 2023, https://doi.org/10.1093/OED/8175480404.

13. Alicestyne Turley, "The Real Story behind 'Aunt Jemima' and a Woman Born Enslaved in Mt. Sterling, Kentucky," *Lexington (KY) Herald-Leader*, June 20, 2023.

14. Frances Price, "'The Hair Tales' Clip: Oprah Shares Being Told by TV News Boss to 'Fix' Her Thick Hair," *Urban Hollywood 411*, October 22, 2022, https://urbanhollywood411.com/the-hair-tales-oprah-shares-hair-story/.

15. Shaun King, "Jack Daniels' Sordid History Shows Cultural Appropriation Is Nothing New—Black Culture Has Been Stolen for Centuries," *New York Daily News,* July 1, 2016, https://www.nydailynews.com/news/national/king -jack-daniels-story-shows-cultural-appropriation-isn-new-article-1.2695808.

16. "How to Avoid Cultural Appropriation and Promote Cultural Awareness Instead," Commisceo Global Consulting, accessed August 26, 2023, https:// www.commisceo-global.com/blog/how-to-avoid-cultural-appropriation -promote-cultural-awareness-instead.

17. Lauren Cover, "How to Spot, Avoid and Learn from Cultural Appropriation in Marketing," Sprout Social, March 1, 2021, https://sproutsocial .com/insights/cultural-appropriation-in-marketing/.

18. Andray Domise, "How to Talk about Cultural Appropriation," *Maclean's*, September 21, 2016, https://macleans.ca/society/how-to-talk-about -cultural-appropriation/.

19. Cover, "How to Spot, Avoid and Learn."

20. Domise, "How to Talk about Cultural Appropriation."

21. Brynn Holland, "The 'Father of Modern Gynecology' Performed Shocking Experiments on Enslaved Women," History (website), updated December 4, 2018, https://www.history.com/news/the-father-of-modern -gynecology-performed-shocking-experiments-on-slaves.

22. Hannah Gaskill, "Judge Weighing Motion to Dismiss Henrietta Lacks' Family Lawsuit against Biotech Firm," *Maryland Matters*, May 17, 2022, https://www.marylandmatters.org/2022/05/17/judge-weighing-motion-to -dismiss-henrietta-lacks-family-lawsuit-against-biotech-firm/.

23. Mary Anne Pazanowski, "Henrietta Lacks' Estate Sues for Profits Derived from Tissue," *Bloomberg Law*, October 5, 2021, https://news .bloomberglaw.com/litigation/henrietta-lacks-estate-sues-for-profits-derived -from-tissue.

24. "About the USPHS Syphilis Study," Tuskegee University, accessed December 26, 2022, https://www.tuskegee.edu/about-us/centers-of-excellence /bioethics-center/about-the-usphs-syphilis-study.

25. Matej Mikulic, "Global Pharmaceutical Industry—Statistics and Facts," Statista, July 14, 2023, https://www.statista.com/topics/1764/global -pharmaceutical-industry/#topicOverview.

26. Walter Rhein, "The Shameful History of Racism in the American Oil Industry," *Cultured*, March 11, 2022, https://readcultured.com/the-shameful -history-of-racism-in-the-american-oil-industry-e7cc8f6aa633.

27. James Grant and Tiana Johnson, "Families of Black Chambers County Farmers Decry Alleged Century-Old Land Theft," *12 News*, Beaumont, TX, July 25, 2021, https://www.12newsnow.com/article/news/local/families-of -black-chambers-county-farmers-rally-for-alleged-century-old-land-theft/502 -c393abcc-9c52-4e4a-8dfb-492c38cb3152.

28. Thomas S. Mulligan and Chris Kraul, "Texaco Settles Race Bias Suit for $176 Million," *Los Angeles Times,* November 16, 1996, https://www.latimes .com/archives/la-xpm-1996-11-16-mn-65290-story.html.

29. Ian Palmer, "Oil and Gas Profits Very High Once Again—What This Feels Like to Energy Consumers," *Forbes*, November 4, 2022, https://www.forbes.com/sites/ianpalmer/2022/11/04/oil-and-gas-profits-very-high-once-again--what-this-feels-like-to-energy-consumers/.

30. "African Americans and the Manhattan Project," Atomic Heritage Foundation, March 1, 2016, https://ahf.nuclearmuseum.org/ahf/history/african-americans-and-manhattan-project/.

31. Melissa Healy, "Charity Patients Irradiated to Gauge Effect on Soldiers," *Los Angeles Times,* January 6, 1994, https://www.latimes.com/archives/la-xpm-1994-01-06-mn-9015-story.html.

32. "Air Pollution from the Oil and Gas Industry," Earthworks, August 18, 2015, https://earthworks.org/resources/fs_oilandgas_airpollution/.

33. Sarah Golden, "How Racism Manifests in Clean Energy," GreenBiz, June 5, 2020, https://www.greenbiz.com/article/how-racism-manifests-clean-energy.

34. Jonathan Lansner, "Black Residents in California Trail in Homeownership, Mortgage Approvals," *Orange County (CA) Register*, January 17, 2022, https://www.ocregister.com/2022/01/17/blacks-in-california-trail-in-homeownership-mortgage-approvals/.

35. Deborah A. Sunter, Sergio Castellanos, and Daniel M. Kammen, "Disparities in Rooftop Photovoltaics Deployment in the United States by Race and Ethnicity," *Nature Sustainability* 2 (2019), https://www.nature.com/articles/s41893-018-0204-z.

36. Emma Foehringer Merchant, "What Is the Clean Energy Industry Doing to Confront Racism?," Greentech Media, October 29, 2020, https://www.greentechmedia.com/articles/read/what-is-the-clean-energy-industry-doing-to-confront-racism.

37. Booker T. Washington, quoted in *Minutes of the University Commission on Southern Race Questions* ([Lexington?], VA: n.p., [between 1917 and 1920]), 29. Available at https://archive.org/details/minutesofunivers00univ/page/28/mode/2up.

Chapter 3: Institutional Reparations

1. "Reconstruction," History (website), updated April 24, 2023, https://www.history.com/topics/american-civil-war/reconstruction.

2. Keri Leigh Merritt, "Land and the Roots of African American Poverty," *Aeon*, March 11, 2016, https://aeon.co/ideas/land-and-the-roots-of-african-american-poverty.

3. This estimate is based on the 4,000 to 5,500 Black beneficiaries of the Southern Homestead Act in Merritt, "Land and the Roots," and the 3,500 beneficiaries in the Great Plains in "African American Homesteaders in the Great Plains," National Park Service, accessed August 26, 2023, https://www.nps.gov/articles/african-american-homesteaders-in-the-great-plains.htm.

4. Becky Little, "How a New Deal Housing Program Enforced Segregation," History (website), updated June 1, 2023, https://www.history.com/news/housing-segregation-new-deal-program.

5. "African Americans and the New Deal," Digital History, accessed June 10, 2022, https://www.digitalhistory.uh.edu/disp_textbook.cfm?smtID=2&psid=3447.

6. Erin Blakemore, "How the GI Bill's Promise Was Denied to a Million Black WWII Veterans," History (website), updated June 21, 2023, https://www.history.com/news/gi-bill-black-wwii-veterans-benefits.

7. Ira Katznelson, "When Is Affirmative Action Fair? On Grievous Harms and Public Remedies," *Social Research* 73, no. 2 (2006): 541–68, http://www.jstor.org/stable/40971835.

8. Nadine Frederique, "COINTELPRO," *Encyclopedia Brittanica,* last updated January 16, 2023, https://www.britannica.com/topic/COINTELPRO.

9. Frederique, "COINTELPRO."

10. David Carr, "Resurrecting a Disgraced Reporter," *New York Times,* October 2, 2014, https://www.nytimes.com/2014/10/05/movies/kill-the-messenger-recalls-a-reporter-wrongly-disgraced.html.

11. Andrew Glass, "Reagan Declares 'War on Drugs,' October 14, 1982," Politico, October 14, 2010, https://www.politico.com/story/2010/10/reagan-declares-war-on-drugs-october-14-1982-043552.

12. Michelle Alexander, *The New Jim Crow: Mass Incarceration in the Age of Colorblindness* (New York: New Press, 2010).

13. Alexander, *New Jim Crow,* 112.

14. Alexander, *New Jim Crow,* 180.

15. Executive Order on Advancing Racial Equity and Support for Underserved Communities through the Federal Government, January 20, 2021, https://www.whitehouse.gov/briefing-room/presidential-actions/2021/01/20/executive-order-advancing-racial-equity-and-support-for-underserved-communities-through-the-federal-government/.

16. "Remarks by Secretary of the Treasury Janet L. Yellen at Inaugural Meeting of Treasury Advisory Committee on Racial Equity," US Department of the Treasury, December 5, 2022, https://home.treasury.gov/news/press-releases/jy1142.

17. La-Brina Almeida, "A History of Racist Federal Housing Policies," Massachusetts Budget and Policy Center, August 6, 2021, https://massbudget.org/2021/08/06/a-history-of-racist-federal-housing-policies/.

18. "How the Property Tax System Harms Black Homeowners and Widens the Racial Wealth Gap," Brookings Institute, August 22, 2023, https://www.brookings.edu/articles/how-the-property-tax-system-harms-black-homeowners-and-widens-the-racial-wealth-gap/#:~:text=Black%20homeowners'%20property%20tax%20burden,of%2021%25%20to%2023%25.

19. "Homeownership Is Much More Costly for Black Homeowners," Housing Matters, March 9, 2022, https://housingmatters.urban.org/research-summary/homeownership-much-more-costly-black-homeowners.

20. "Homeownership Rate by Race," Bankrate (website), accessed August 26, 2023, https://www.bankrate.com/homeownership/home-ownership-statistics/#rates-by-race-and-ethnicity.

21. Stuart M. Butler and Jonathan Grabinsky, "Tackling the Legacy of Persistent Urban Inequality and Concentrated Poverty," Brookings Institution, November 16, 2020, https://www.brookings.edu/blog/up-front/2020/11/16/tackling-the-legacy-of-persistent-urban-inequality-and-concentrated-poverty/.

22. "African Americans and the New Deal," Digital History, accessed June 10, 2022, https://www.digitalhistory.uh.edu/disp_textbook.cfm?smtID=2&psid=3447.

23. Vann R. Newkirk II, "The Great Land Robbery," *Atlantic,* September 2019, https://www.theatlantic.com/magazine/archive/2019/09/this-land-was-our-land/594742/.

24. Newkirk, "Great Land Robbery."

25. Ellen Terrell, "National Recovery Administration (NRA) and the New Deal: A Resource Guide," Library of Congress, updated July 1, 2020, https://guides.loc.gov/national-recovery-administration.

26. Mary-Elizabeth B. Murphy, "African Americans in the Great Depression and New Deal," *Oxford Research Encyclopedia of American History,* November 19, 2020, https://doi.org/10.1093/acrefore/9780199329175.013.632.

27. Larry DeWitt, "The Decision to Exclude Agricultural and Domestic Workers from the 1935 Social Security Act," *Social Security Bulletin* 70, no. 4 (2010), https://www.ssa.gov/policy/docs/ssb/v70n4/v70n4p49.html.

28. Liam Dillon and Ben Poston, "The Racist History of America's Interstate Highway Boom," *Los Angeles Times,* November 11, 2021, https://www.latimes.com/homeless-housing/story/2021-11-11/the-racist-history-of-americas-interstate-highway-boom.

29. Rachael Dottle, Laura Bliss, and Pablo Robles, "What It Looks Like to Reconnect Black Communities Torn Apart by Highways," Bloomberg, July 28, 2021, https://www.bloomberg.com/graphics/2021-urban-highways-infrastructure-racism/.

30. Jennifer Epstein and Josh Wingrove, "Buttigieg Says U.S. Will Use Infrastructure Bill to Address Racist Highway Design," Bloomberg, November 8, 2021, https://www.bloomberg.com/news/articles/2021-11-08/buttigieg-targets-racist-road-design-with-public-works-bill.

31. Brent Cebul, "Tearing Down Black America," *Boston Review,* July 22, 2020, https://bostonreview.net/articles/brent-cebul-tearing-down-black-america/.

32. Mindy Thompson Fullilove, "Root Shock: The Consequences of African American Dispossession," *Journal of Urban Health: Bulletin of the New York Academy of Medicine* 78, no. 1 (March 2001): 78.

33. Greg Bluestein, "Why Monday Is No Longer Confederate Memorial Day in Georgia," *Atlanta Journal-Constitution,* April 22, 2018, https://www.ajc.com/blog/politics/why-monday-longer-confederate-memorial-day-georgia/55scplUOZWOIbAzmMKZnXM/.

34. Blakemore, "GI Bill's Promise Was Denied."

35. Blakemore, "GI Bill's Promise Was Denied."

36. Victoria Ebner, "Veterans Affairs Has Denied Benefits to Black People at Higher Rates for Years, Lawsuit Alleges," CNBC, November 28, 2022, https://www.cnbc.com/2022/11/28/veterans-affairs-has-denied-benefits-to-black -people-at-higher-rates-for-years-lawsuit-alleges.html.

37. Ebner, "Veterans Affairs Has Denied Benefits."

38. "78 Percent of Union Veterans Affairs Employees Surveyed Say Racism Is a Problem at the VA," American Federation of Government Employees, August 7, 2020, https://www.afge.org/publication/78-percent-of-union-veterans -affairs-employees-surveyed-say-racism-is-a-problem-at-the-va/.

39. "78 Percent of Employees Surveyed."

40. Rebecca Kheel, "Racial Disparities in VA Benefits Advocates Say Are Rampant Set to Get Watchdog Probe," Military.com, November 30, 2021, https://www.military.com/daily-news/2021/11/30/racial-disparities-va-benefits -advocates-say-are-rampant-set-get-watchdog-probe.html.

41. Christopher S. Chivvis and Sahil Lauji, "Diversity in the High Brass," Carnegie Endowment for International Peace, September 6, 2022, https:// carnegieendowment.org/2022/09/06/diversity-in-high-brass-pub-87694.

42. Chivvis and Lauji, "Diversity in the High Brass."

43. Chivvis and Lauji, "Diversity in the High Brass."

44. Curran McSwigan, "Shut Out: The Dearth of Opportunity for Minority Contracting," Third Way, June 23, 2022, https://www.thirdway.org/report/shut -out-the-dearth-of-opportunity-for-minority-contracting.

45. "Race and Ethnicity," Prison Policy Initiative, updated September 1, 2023, https://www.prisonpolicy.org/research/race_and_ethnicity/.

46. "South Carolina Civil Forfeiture Disproportionately Targets Black Men," Equal Justice Initiative, March 4, 2019, https://eji.org/news/south-carolina -civil-forfeiture-disproportionately-targets-black-men/.

47. "South Carolina Civil Forfeiture."

48. Joan Oleck, "With 40,000 Americans Incarcerated for Marijuana Offenses, the Cannabis Industry Needs to Step Up, Activists Said This Week," Forbes, June 26, 2020, https://www.forbes.com/sites/joanoleck/2020/06/26 /with-40000-americans-incarcerated-for-marijuana-offenses-the-cannabis -industry-needs-to-step-up-activists-said-this-week/.

49. "Marijuana Legality by State," DISA Global Solutions, updated August 1, 2023, https://disa.com/map-of-marijuana-legality-by-state.

50. Christy Visher and John Eason, "A Better Path Forward for Criminal Justice: Changing Prisons to Help People Change," Brookings Institution, April 2021, https://www.brookings.edu/articles/a-better-path-forward-for-criminal -justice-changing-prisons-to-help-people-change/.

51. Visher and Eason, "Better Path Forward."

52. Robert Martinson, "What Works? Questions and Answers about Prison Reform," Public Interest 35 (Spring 1974): 22–54.

53. Gordon B. Dahl and Magne Mogstad, "The Benefits of Rehabilitative Incarceration," Reporter 1 (March 2020), https://www.nber.org/reporter/2020 number1/benefits-rehabilitative-incarceration.

54. Wendy Sawyer, "Visualizing the Racial Disparities in Mass Incarceration," Prison Policy Initiative, July 27, 2020, https://www.prison policy.org/blog/2020/07/27/disparities/.

55. "Opposing Mandatory Minimums," Equal Justice under Law, accessed August 28, 2023, https://equaljusticeunderlaw.org/mandatory-minimums-1.

56. "Opposing Mandatory Minimums."

57. "Facts and Case Summary—Batson v. Kentucky," United States Courts (website), accessed August 28, 2023, https://www.uscourts.gov/educational -resources/educational-activities/facts-and-case-summary-batson-v-kentucky.

58. "Race and the Jury: Illegal Discrimination in Jury Selection," Equal Justice Initiative, accessed July 5, 2022, https://eji.org/report/race-and-the-jury/.

59. "Race and the Jury."

60. Ashley Nellis, "The Color of Justice: Racial and Ethnic Disparity in State Prisons," Sentencing Project, October 13, 2021, https://www.sentencing project.org/reports/the-color-of-justice-racial-and-ethnic-disparity-in-state -prisons-the-sentencing-project/.

61. Nicole Lewis, Anna Flagg, and Aviva Shen, "What 2,392 Incarcerated People Think about #DefundThePolice," Marshall Project, October 27, 2020, https://www.themarshallproject.org/2020/10/27/what-2-392-incarcerated -people-think-about-defundthepolice.

62. Libby Stanford, "Which States Offer Universal Pre-K? It's More Complicated Than You Might Think," *EducationWeek,* January 25, 2023, https://www.edweek.org/teaching-learning/which-states-offer-universal-pre-k -its-more-complicated-than-you-might-think/2023/01.

63. Russell Brooker, "The Education of Black Children in the Jim Crow South," America's Black Holocaust Museum, accessed January 5, 2023, https:// www.abhmuseum.org/education-for-blacks-in-the-jim-crow-south/.

64. Laura Meckler, "Study Finds Black and Latino Students Face Significant 'Funding Gap,'" *Washington Post,* July 22, 2020, https://www.washingtonpost .com/education/study-finds-black-and-latino-students-face-significant-funding -gap/2020/07/21/712f376a-caca-11ea-b0e3-d55bda07d66a_story.html.

65. Gary Orfield and Danielle Jarvie, "Black Segregation Matters: School Resegregation and Black Educational Opportunity," UCLA Civil Rights Project, December 2020, https://www.civilrightsproject.ucla.edu/research /k-12-education/integration-and-diversity/black-segregation-matters-school -resegregation-and-black-educational-opportunity/BLACK-SEGREGATION -MATTERS-final-121820.pdf.

66. Warren Fiske, "PolitiFact VA: Public Schools Are More Segregated Now Than in the Late 1960s," VPM, June 8, 2022, https://vpm.org/news /articles/32806/politifact-va-public-schools-are-more-segregated-now-than -in-the-late-1960s.

67. "Addressing the Lasting Impacts of Racist Choices on Virginia's Education System," Commonwealth Institute for Fiscal Analysis, accessed August 28, 2023, https://thecommonwealthinstitute.org/research/modern-day -segregation-addressing-lasting-impacts/3/.

68. Nancy MacLean, "'School Choice' Developed as a Way to Protect Segregation and Abolish Public Schools," *Washington Post,* September 27, 2021, https://www.washingtonpost.com/outlook/2021/09/27/school-choice -developed-way-protect-segregation-abolish-public-schools/.

69. Alan Rodriguez Espinoza, "School Segregation Is Worsening in Virginia, Studies Find," VPM, November 12, 2020, https://www.vpm.org/news/2020-11 -12/school-segregation-is-worsening-in-virginia-studies-find.

70. Espinoza, "School Segregation Worsening in Virginia."

71. Susan Adams and Hank Tucker, "How America Cheated Its Black Colleges," *Forbes,* February 1, 2022, https://www.forbes.com/sites/susan adams/2022/02/01/for-hbcus-cheated-out-of-billions-bomb-threats-are-latest -indignity/.

72. Victoria M. Massie, "White Women Benefit Most from Affirmative Action—and Are among Its Fiercest Opponents," Vox, updated May 25, 2016, https://www.vox.com/2016/5/25/11682950/fisher-supreme-court-white -women-affirmative-action.

73. Andrew Brandt, "Business of Football: The Supreme Court Sends a Message to the NCAA," *Sports Illustrated,* June 29, 2021, https://www.si.com /nfl/2021/06/29/business-of-football-supreme-court-unanimous-ruling.

74. Natalie Moore, "Contract Buying Robbed Black Families in Chicago of Billions," WBEZ, Chicago, May 30, 2019, https://www.npr.org/local /309/2019/05/30/728122642/contract-buying-robbed-black-families-in -chicago-of-billions.

75. Yuliya Parshina-Kottas et al.,"What the Tulsa Race Massacre Destroyed," *New York Times,* May 24, 2021, https://www.nytimes.com /interactive/2021/05/24/us/tulsa-race-massacre.html.

76. "History of Lynching in America," NAACP, accessed July 14, 2022, https://naacp.org/find-resources/history-explained/history-lynching-america.

77. Equal Justice Initiative, "Lynching in America: Confronting the Legacy of Racial Terror," 3rd ed. (Montgomery, AL: Equal Justice Initiative, 2017), https://eji.org/reports/lynching-in-america/.

78. "Justice for United States Victims of State Sponsored Terrorism Act: Eligibility and Funding," Congressional Research Service, updated April 11, 2023, https://crsreports.congress.gov/product/pdf/IF/IF10341.

79. Dalton Conley, "The Cost of Slavery," *New York Times,* February 15, 2003, https://www.nytimes.com/2003/02/15/opinion/the-cost-of-slavery.html.

80. Rashawn Ray, "Why Is It So Hard for America to Designate Domestic Terrorism and Hate Crimes?," Brookings Institution, March 18, 2021, https:// www.brookings.edu/blog/how-we-rise/2021/03/18/why-is-it-so-hard-for -america-to-designate-domestic-terrorism-and-hate-crimes/.

81. "Health Disparities between Blacks and Whites Run Deep," Harvard T. H. Chan School of Public Health, accessed December 28, 2022, https:// www.hsph.harvard.edu/news/hsph-in-the-news/health-disparities-between -blacks-and-whites-run-deep/; Latoya Hill and Samantha Artiga, "What Is Driving Widening Racial Disparities in Life Expectancy?," KFF, May 23,

2023, https://www.kff.org/racial-equity-and-health-policy/issue-brief/what
-is-driving-widening-racial-disparities-in-life-expectancy/.

82. Jazz Keyes, "Slave Food: The Impact of Unhealthy Eating Habits on
the Black Community," *Ebony,* June 18, 2019, https://www.ebony.com/black
-health-food-diet/.

83. Peter Urban, "Minorities Spend Less on Health Care than Whites,"
AARP, August 23, 2021, https://www.aarp.org/health/conditions-treatments
/info-2021/minorities-health-care-spending.html.

84. Urban, "Minorities Spend Less."

85. Samantha Artiga, Latoya Hill, and Anthony Damico, "Health Coverage
by Race and Ethnicity, 2010–2021," KFF, December 20, 2022, https://www
.kff.org/racial-equity-and-health-policy/issue-brief/health-coverage-by-race
-and-ethnicity/.

86. "Facts about the U.S. Black Population," Pew Research, March 2,
2023, https://www.pewresearch.org/social-trends/fact-sheet/facts-about-the-us
-black-population/.

87. Maia Mulko, "Black Doctors Who Made History in Medicine,"
Interesting Engineering, February 19, 2022, https://interestingengineering.com
/lists/black-doctors-medicine.

88. Alaina G. Levine, "Profiles in Versatility: Physicist to Test Nanoparticle-
and-Laser Cancer Treatment in Humans," *APS News* 31, no. 9 (October 2022),
https://www.aps.org/publications/apsnews/202210/profiles.cfm.

89. Darcell P. Scharff et al., "More Than Tuskegee: Understanding Mistrust
about Research Participation," National Library of Medicine, August 2010,
https://www.ncbi.nlm.nih.gov/pmc/articles/PMC4354806/.

90. "Joint Center Report Highlights Deep Inequity in Broadband Access
across the Black Rural South," Joint Center for Political and Economic Studies,
October 6, 2021, https://jointcenter.org/joint-center-report-highlights-deep
-inequity-in-broadband-access-across-the-black-rural-south/.

91. James K. Willcox, "Infrastructure Law Includes $65 Billion for
Improving Internet Access," *Consumer Reports,* updated November 15,
2021, https://www.consumerreports.org/internet/infrastructure-bill-includes
-65-billion-for-internet-access-a6861027212/.

92. "What Is Environmental Racism?," *Medical News Today*, updated February
15, 2023, https://www.medicalnewstoday.com/articles/environmental-racism.

93. Phil McKenna, "EPA Finds Black Americans Face More Health-
Threatening Air Pollution," Inside Climate News, March 2, 2018, https://
insideclimatenews.org/news/02032018/air-pollution-data-african-american-race
-health-epa-research/.

94. "What Is Environmental Racism?"

95. "What Is Soil Pollution?," Environmental Pollution Centers, accessed
January 18, 2023, https://www.environmentalpollutioncenters.org/soil/;
Monisha Jaishankar et al., "Toxicity, Mechanism and Health Effects of Some
Heavy Metals," National Library of Medicine, November 15, 2014, https://
www.ncbi.nlm.nih.gov/pmc/articles/PMC4427717/.

96. Victoria St. Martin and Aydali Campa, "Study: Higher Concentrations of Arsenic, Uranium in Drinking Water in Black, Latino, Indigenous Communities," Inside Climate News, December 27, 2022, https://insideclimatenews.org/news/27122022/study-higher-concentrations-of-arsenic-uranium-in-drinking-water-in-black-latino-indigenous-communities/.

97. "New Drinking Water Report: Communities of Color More Likely to Suffer Drinking Water Violations for Years," Natural Resources Defense Council, September 24, 2019, https://www.nrdc.org/press-releases/new-drinking-water-report-communities-color-more-likely-suffer-drinking-water.

98. "Inhalable Particulate Matter and Health (PM2.5 and PM10)," California Air Resources Board, accessed January 13, 2023, https://ww2.arb.ca.gov/resources/inhalable-particulate-matter-and-health.

99. "Inhalable Particulate Matter."

100. M. Sophia Newman, "Why Racial Disparities in Asthma Are an Urban Planning Issue," Next City, May 20, 2019, https://nextcity.org/features/why-racial-disparities-in-asthma-are-an-urban-planning-issue.

101. "Noise Pollution More Common in Communities of Color and Racially Segregated Cities," Harvard T. H. Chan School of Public Health, 2017, https://www.hsph.harvard.edu/news/hsph-in-the-news/noise-pollution-segregated-cities/.

102. "Radioactive Waste," US Environmental Protection Agency, updated August 16, 2023, https://www.epa.gov/radtown/radioactive-waste.

103. "Radioactive Substances and Their Impact on Health," Reuters, March 24, 2011, https://www.reuters.com/article/us-radioactive-health-idUSTRE72N6LJ20110324.

104. Kim A. Angelon-Gaetz, David B. Richardson, and Steve Wing, "Inequalities in the Nuclear Age: Impact of Race and Gender on Radiation Exposure at the Savannah River Site (1951–1999)," National Library of Medicine, January 2013, https://www.ncbi.nlm.nih.gov/pmc/articles/PMC3534859/.

105. Marilyn Vann, testimony to the US Senate Committee on Indian Affairs Oversight Hearing on Select Provisions of the 1866 Reconstruction Treaties Indian Affairs between the United States and Oklahoma Indian Tribes, July 27, 2022, https://www.indian.senate.gov/sites/default/files/7%2025%202022%20%20Ms.%20Vann%20FINAL%20Freedman%20Testimony.pdf.

106. Vann testimony.

107. "Confederacy Signs Treaties with Native Americans," History (website), updated July 9, 2021, https://www.history.com/this-day-in-history/confederacy-signs-treaties-with-native-americans.

108. American Civil War Research Database (website), accessed September 2, 2022, http://www.civilwardata.com/dbstatus.html.

109. Congresswoman Maxine Waters, testimony to the US Senate Committee on Indian Affairs, in "Chairwoman Waters Testifies before Senate on Need to Uphold Equal Citizenship Rights of Descendants of Freedmen: 'We Must

Honor Our Word as a Nation,'" US House Committee on Financial Services Democrats, July 28, 2022, https://democrats-financialservices.house.gov/news /documentsingle.aspx?DocumentID=409713.

110. Charles Cochran, *Congressional Record,* January 15, 1903, quoted in "History," US Department of Commerce, https://www.commerce.gov/about /history.

111. Rebecca Leppert, "A Look at Black-Owned Businesses in the U.S.," Pew Research Center, February 21, 2023, https://www.pewresearch.org/short -reads/2023/02/21/a-look-at-black-owned-businesses-in-the-u-s/.

112. Tracy Jan, "Minority-Owned Firms Report Tougher Time Accessing Credit than White Firms," *Washington Post,* November 8, 2017, https:// www.washingtonpost.com/news/wonk/wp/2017/11/08/minority-owned-firms -report-tougher-time-accessing-credit-than-white-firms/.

113. Jan, "Minority-Owned Firms."

114. Leppert, "A Look at Black-Owned Businesses."

115. Spectra Myers and Pamela Chan, "Stuck from the Start: The Financial Challenges of Low- and Moderate-Income African-American Entrepreneurs in the South," Prosperity Now, July 2017, https://prosperitynow.org/sites/default /files/PDFs/07-2017_stuck_from_the_start.pdf.

116. Emma Sapong, "Roots of Tension: Race, Hair, Competition and Black Beauty Stores," April 25, 2017, Minnesota Public Radio, https://www.mprnews .org/story/2017/04/25/black-beauty-shops-korean-suppliers-roots-of-tension-mn.

117. Eliza Anyangwe, "Why Is Africa So Poor? You Asked Google—Here's the Answer," *Guardian,* June 28, 2017, https://www.theguardian.com /commentisfree/2017/jun/28/why-africa-so-poor-google.

118. Anyangwe, "Why Is Africa So Poor?"

119. "Voting Laws Roundup: October 2021," Brennan Center for Justice, October 4, 2021, https://www.brennancenter.org/our-work/research-reports /voting-laws-roundup-october-2021.

Chapter 4: Spiritual Reparations

1. Jemar Tisby, *The Color of Compromise* (Grand Rapids: Zondervan, 2019).

2. Frank Smith, *The History of the Presbyterian Church in America: The Continuing Church Movement* (Manassas, VA: Reformation Educational Foundation, 1985), 3.

3. Tisby, *Color of Compromise,* 52.

4. James Henley Thornwell, "Relation of the Church to Slavery," in *The Collected Writings of James Henley Thornwell,* vol. 4, *Ecclesiastical* (Richmond: Presbyterian Committee of Publication, 1873), 383.

5. Henry Noble Sherwood, "The Formation of the American Colonization Society," *Journal of Negro History* 2, no. 3 (July 1917): 214.

6. Mark A. Noll, *The Civil War as a Theological Crisis* (Chapel Hill: University of North Carolina Press, 2006), 39.

7. Tisby, *Color of Compromise*, 94.

8. Tisby, *Color of Compromise*, 96.

9. Juan O. Sánchez, *Religion and the Ku Klux Klan: Biblical Appropriation in Their Literature and Songs* (Jefferson, NC: McFarland, 2016), 14–15.

10. Walter Carl Wright, *Religious and Patriotic Ideals of the Ku Klux Klan* (Waco, TX: self-pub., 1926).

11. DeNeen L. Brown, "The Preacher Who Used Christianity to Revive the Ku Klux Klan," *Washington Post,* April 10, 2018, https://www.washingtonpost.com/news/retropolis/wp/2018/04/08/the-preacher-who-used-christianity-to-revive-the-ku-klux-klan/.

12. Jerrolyn Eulinberg, *A Lynched Black Wall Street: A Womanist Perspective on Terrorism, Religion, and Black Resilience in the 1921 Tulsa Race Massacre* (Eugene, OR: Cascade, 2021), 182.

13. Martin Luther King Jr., *Letter from Birmingham Jail* (1963; repr., London: Penguin Books, 2018).

14. See Exod. 3:20–22 and 11:1–3.

15. Matthew Schlimm, "Saving the Egyptians," *Christian Century*, January 12, 2022, referencing Duke L. Kwon and Gregory Thompson, *Reparations: A Christian Call for Repentance and Repair* (Grand Rapids: Brazos, 2021).

16. Schlimm, "Saving the Egyptians."

17. Schlimm, "Saving the Egyptians."